HUMBLE INFLUENCE

The Strength of True Followership

By Jim Matuga

Published in the United States of America by

**SPIRIT MEDIA**

Spirit Media Inc
https://spiritmedia.us

Spirit Media and our logos are trademarks of
Spirit Media Inc
8045 Arco Corporate Drive STE 130
Raleigh, NC 27617
1 (888) 800-3744

Religion & Spirituality | Christian Books & Bibles | Spiritual Growth
Paperback ISBN: 979-8-89307-144-3
Harback ISBN: 979-8-89307-150-4
eBook ISBN: 979-8-89307-148-1
PDF ISBN: 979-8-89307-149-8
Discussion Guide PDF ISBN: 979-8-89307-151-1
Library of Congress Control Number: 2025909799

ABOUT THE COVER

In *Humble Influence: The Strength of True Followership*, Jim Matuga beautifully illustrates how true leadership is often shaped by strong, intentional followership—much like a school of fish instinctively moving together in harmony. Just as fish rely on their leader to navigate currents, avoid danger, and find sustenance, effective followers support, elevate, and empower their leaders to achieve a shared vision. The single white fish leading the red school on the book's cover symbolizes how influence flows not from authority but from trust, unity, and purposeful collaboration. This book redefines the power of followership as an essential force in leadership and success.

CONTENTS

ACKNOWLEDGEMENTS

Writing *Humble Influence* has been one of the most meaningful journeys of my life. This message was born from years of reflection, conversation, prayer, and the faithful presence of people who embodied the very truths I've attempted to capture in this book.

I want to thank those who challenged me, encouraged me, and walked with me through the process. Your support has been a form of humble influence in my life.

To my family—thank you for your love, patience, and constant encouragement.

To the mentors and friends who showed me what it means to be a servant-hearted follower—your example shaped every page.

To the team at InnerAction Media— especially Dylan and Brian - your belief in this message helped bring it to life.

Special thanks to:

My wife, partner and biggest encourager Rebekah, Matt, Jay, James, Andy, Bruce, Frank, John, Kevin and Nick.

And to "followers' everywhere striving to lead from the middle, to serve quietly, and to influence with humility—this message is for you.

With deepest gratitude,

Jim Matuga

WHY I WROTE
THIS BOOK...

In a bustling coffee shop in the heart of New York City, I sat across from a young professional named Michael. He'd landed his dream job at a prominent tech firm, but he felt lost.

"I want to make an impact," he said, stirring his coffee absentmindedly. "But I'm not a leader. Everyone talks about leadership, but what about people like me? I don't want to be in charge—I just want to do great work."

That conversation was the spark for this book. Michael wasn't alone. Over the years, I've met countless individuals who feel overshadowed by the leadership narrative. They're the ones working tirelessly behind the scenes, driving success without seeking the limelight.

This book is for them—for you. It's about redefining success and celebrating the vital role of followership.

When I first set out to write this book, I asked myself a simple question; Why do we celebrate leaders so often, yet rarely acknowledge the followers who make their success possible?

For years, I had been immersed in the world of leadership—reading books, attending seminars, and studying the habits of great leaders. Leadership, it seemed, was the ultimate skill to master, the key to unlocking success in life and business.

But as I reflected on my own experiences, I realized something profound: leadership cannot exist without followership.

Think about it. The most celebrated leaders in history—whether they're biblical figures like Moses, visionaries like Martin Luther

King Jr., or modern trailblazers like Elon Musk—achieved greatness not by standing alone, but through the collective efforts of those who supported and followed them. These followers were not passive or unimportant. They were active participants, critical thinkers, and indispensable contributors.

Yet, followership is often misunderstood. It's seen as a secondary role, a fallback for those who don't aspire to lead. Nothing could be further from the truth. Followership is a skill, a mindset, and a powerful force. Great followers drive missions forward, support their leaders, and create the foundation for success.

In today's fast-paced and interconnected world, the importance of followership is gaining recognition as a critical factor in organizational success. Adam Hanft's December, 15, 2024 Inc. Article: *Why Followership Is More Important Than Ever*, explores this often-overlooked role and highlights how followers can shape outcomes, influence leaders, and drive teams toward their goals.

Hanft challenges the traditional leadership narrative, pointing out that in a modern environment marked by collaboration, complexity, and innovation, followership is not a passive act but an active, intentional process. This perspective aligns perfectly with the principles outlined in *Humble Influence: The Strength of True Followership*.

Hanft's insights draw attention to the shift happening across industries: leaders are no longer the sole architects of success. Today's most effective teams rely on followers who take initiative, offer ideas, and hold themselves accountable.

This redefinition mirrors the foundational ideas of Robert Kelley's 1992, *The Power of Followership*, which was among the first to argue that great followers are characterized by their engagement, critical thinking, and ability to partner effectively with leaders. Kelley identified that organizations thrive not because of "sheepish" obedience, but because of proactive individuals who embrace responsibility and align their actions with a shared purpose.

The parallels between Hanft's modern observations and the lessons of humility in followership outlined in *Humble Influence* are striking. While Hanft points to the necessity of shifting away from outdated leader-centric models, *Humble Influence* takes this idea further by demonstrating how humility, empathy, and adaptability are the cornerstones of great followership. Followers who prioritize the team's success over personal accolades—those who listen, contribute, and strengthen the leader's vision—are indispensable in achieving lasting results.

The concepts explored in Hanft's article resonate throughout this book. *Humble Influence* builds on the belief that followership is not simply "supporting" leadership; it is about amplifying it. By aligning personal values with the team's mission and intentionally embracing the role of follower, individuals elevate their teams and their leaders.

As Hanft aptly notes, the challenges of today demand a more dynamic understanding of leadership and followership—one where leaders and followers act as partners, collaborating to overcome obstacles and achieve shared goals.

This is the essence of *Humble Influence*, that true greatness lies not just in leading well, but in following with purpose, humility, and a commitment to something greater than oneself.

This book is a celebration of followership. It's a guide for those who recognize that being a follower is not about subservience but about partnership. It's for the quiet contributors, the team players, and the behind-the-scenes problem-solvers who know that their work matters just as much—if not more—than the person at the top.

In the chapters that follow, you'll discover the principles of effective followership, drawn from history, biblical wisdom, and real-world examples. You'll learn how to align with your purpose, cultivate trust, and take initiative in ways that elevate your leader, your team, and yourself.

This is not a book about stepping out of the shadows. It's about understanding the transformative power of the role you already play.

It's about embracing the idea that followership is not just a precursor to leadership—it's an art and a calling in its own right.

I hope this book inspires you to see followership in a new light and empowers you to lead from within. Because at the heart of every great success story is a team of great followers—and you are one of them.

Welcome to *Humble Influence: The Strength of True Followership*

Jim Matuga

WHAT THIS BOOK IS ABOUT...

Followership is often misunderstood. The idea of being a follower can be seen as a secondary role reserved for those who don't aspire to lead. I argue that *nothing* could be further from the truth. True followership is an art—an active, intentional process of aligning with a mission, supporting leaders, and contributing to collective success. It requires humility to serve, courage to speak up, and wisdom to act with purpose. It is the strength of true followership that matters. Just as Joshua's years of faithful service under Moses prepared him to lead the Israelites into the Promised Land, your own season of followership is not a waiting room—it's a crucible for growth. In these moments of learning, observing, and contributing, you are not standing in the shadows; you are forging the skills and character that will one day define your legacy.

Humble Influence is the ability to positively impact a team, organization, or leader through trust, dedication, and service—without needing a formal leadership role. It means following with purpose, taking initiative, supporting the vision, and contributing ideas while remaining teachable and adaptable. A follower with humble influence doesn't seek recognition but instead uplifts the team, fosters collaboration, and helps create an environment where everyone can succeed.

"Good followership is a prerequisite for good leadership."
—John C. Maxwell

In 1998, John C. Maxwell published *The 21 Irrefutable Laws of Leadership*, a book that became a New York Times bestseller and has since sold nearly two million copies. It not only resonated with aspiring leaders worldwide but also launched an entire industry dedicated to the study and practice of leadership. Today, the "business of leadership" spans books, conferences, graduate programs, and online courses, generating over $50 billion annually.

This explosion of interest in leadership is no surprise. Leadership is aspirational—many people see themselves as potential leaders. But what about those who don't aspire to lead? What about the followers? Those are the questions I began to ask myself on April 17, 2007, while attending a leadership conference at West Virginia University. That day, I heard author James Kouzes speak about his book, *The Leadership Challenge*. And that's where the idea for this book first was planted in my mind. It only took 18 years of experience, conversations, study, research and clarifying my thoughts to finally gain the courage to actually put words to my ideas.

My value proposition was this: Where can someone who prefers to work behind the scenes—who values contribution over command—turn for guidance and training?

Surprisingly, resources for followers are scarce. While leadership programs abound, materials aimed at helping individuals grow as followers are almost nonexistent. This gap is striking, especially given that the success of any leader hinges on the effectiveness of their followers.

Do you see the paradox?

For nearly three decades, I've been privileged to work with extraordinary leaders and mentors—people like Milan Puskar, founder of Mylan Laboratories; Doug Leech, founder of Centra Bank; and yes, even John Maxwell himself. Their wisdom, guidance, and generosity taught me the nuances of effective leadership.

Over the course of my 36-year business career, I've talked with thousands of business leaders. Since 2017, I've interviewed hundreds of business owners and leaders on my weekly podcast "Positively West Virginia." And each episode I ask these leaders about their thoughts on leadership. What I found is the universal truth that everything rises and falls on leadership.

But I've also observed another truth: as much as leadership requires training, *followership requires it just as much.* It's not enough to be a leader of vision and charisma. A leader without effective followers is like a captain with no crew.

"He who thinks he leads, but has no
followers, is only taking a walk."
—John C. Maxwell

Followership, contrary to popular belief, isn't about passively "doing what you're told." It's an active, intentional role that demands discipline, critical thinking, and emotional intelligence. Yet society often overlooks its significance, assuming that following is easy or innate. This assumption is wrong.

Great followership is as much a skill as great leadership. It requires: *humility* to serve without seeking the spotlight, *courage* to challenge decisions respectfully when necessary, *loyalty* to the mission and the leader- even during difficult times, and *proactivity* to take initiative and contribute meaningfully.

Throughout history, we've seen the impact of effective followership through humble influence:

Joshua served under Moses for 40 years before leading the Israelites to the Promised Land.

Elisha followed Elijah for a decade before continuing his mentor's prophetic legacy.

Alexander the Great followed his teacher Aristotle, whose philosophies shaped his strategies as a world-changing leader.

Helen Keller followed her teacher Anne Sullivan, whose guidance helped her overcome immense challenges and become a renowned author and activist.

The Apostle Peter followed Jesus, learning from His teachings and example, before becoming the cornerstone of the early church.

Mahatma Gandhi followed the teachings of nonviolent leaders like Leo Tolstoy, which influenced his philosophy of peaceful resistance that reshaped India's fight for independence.

Florence Nightingale followed the guidance of her mentors in statistics and medicine, which equipped her to revolutionize modern nursing.

Ruth followed Naomi, demonstrating loyalty and faith, ultimately becoming part of the lineage of King David and Jesus Christ.

In contrast, history's worst leaders often failed because they never learned to follow. Tyranny, dysfunction, and failure often result when leaders lack the humility and empathy developed through followership. *This book is about changing that narrative.*

The goal isn't to diminish leadership—it's to elevate followership. Effective followership isn't about blind obedience or subservience. It's about being an active participant in the mission, a trusted partner to your leader, and a contributor to the greater good. It's about knowing when to support, when to challenge, and how to ensure the success of the entire organization.

In the Holy Bible, Romans 13:1 (NIV) states, *"Let everyone be subject to the governing authorities, for there is no authority except that which God has established. The authorities that exist have been established by God."*

This verse highlights the biblical foundation of followership, reminding us that submission to leadership is an act of faith and trust in God's divine order. Great followers recognize that their role is not one of passive compliance but of active, respectful support for those in authority. By embracing humility, obedience, and a servant's heart, followers contribute to the success of their leaders and the missions entrusted to them. True followership, as exemplified in this scripture, is about honoring God's design for leadership and influence, knowing that even in following, there is strength, purpose, and opportunity to reflect Christ-like character.

Over the years, I've seen the need for a roadmap—something to guide people in becoming the best followers they can be. Whether at work, at home, in community organizations, or on sports teams, followership is the thread that ties all aspects of life together. That's why I wrote this book.

Here, you'll find the principles of followership distilled from history- biblical and world, psychology, and real-world experiences, and some not-so real experiences. You'll learn how to develop the skills and mindset of an effective follower and how these lessons prepare you for leadership when the time comes.

Because at the heart of every great leader is a follower who once listened, observed, and grew. And at the heart of every successful organization is a team of followers working with purpose, passion, and partnership.

In writing this book, it also became evident to me that these principles are timeless. Jesus Christ of Nazareth is celebrated as arguably the greatest leader of all time, yet His unparalleled leadership was deeply rooted in His extraordinary ability to follow.

Throughout His life, Jesus demonstrated perfect obedience and submission to the will of God the Father, often stating, *"For I have come down from heaven not to do my will but to do the will of him who sent me."* (John 6:38 NIV).

Jesus was at once - the greatest leader of all time, but also the greatest follower of all time. This humble alignment with a higher purpose exemplified the essence of true followership: trust, faith, and unwavering commitment. Jesus followed God's plan even to the point of self-sacrifice and death on a cross, modeling servanthood, humility, and love as the foundation of leadership. By living as both the ultimate follower and leader, Jesus redefined greatness—not as a quest for power, but as a journey of service, showing that to lead well, one must first follow faithfully.

Welcome to the journey. Let's redefine followership together.

"Leadership
and learning are
indispensable
to each other."
—John F. Kennedy

CHAPTER 1: THE IMPORTANCE OF FOLLOWING

"Before you can lead, you must learn to follow."

One of my mentors, Mr. Doug, said these words to me during my early days as a budding entrepreneur. At the time, I dismissed the idea, believing leadership was about charisma, vision, and authority—not about following someone else's direction.

Then one day, he handed me a Bible and opened it to the book of Joshua.

Joshua is celebrated as one of the greatest leaders in history. He led the Israelites into the Promised Land, brought down the walls of Jericho, and secured a legacy of courage and faith. But Joshua's leadership journey didn't begin with a command. It began with *obedience, patience, and years of followership.* For 40 years, Joshua served under Moses, a towering figure who spoke with God and led the Israelites out of Egypt. Joshua wasn't merely a spectator—he was actively learning and contributing. He led battles, carried out Moses' instructions, and served as his right hand. Most importantly, he observed Moses' leadership: the triumphs, the challenges, and even the mistakes. Joshua's transformation from follower to leader wasn't instant or glamorous. It was forged in the wilderness, through years of faithfulness and service.

"Great leaders don't just appear," Mr. Doug said, closing the Bible. "They are forged through followership."

At the time, I was hungry to lead. I wanted to take charge, implement my ideas, and make a name for myself. But my mentor's words challenged me. Could it be that following was just as important as leading?

The story of Joshua shows us that followership is not a lesser role—it is a *preparation for greatness.* Following teaches discipline, empathy, and the humility needed to guide others effectively. Joshua learned this the hard way. When Moses sent twelve spies to scout the Promised Land, only two—Joshua and Caleb—returned with faith that the Israelites could conquer it. The others spread fear and doubt, derailing the mission. Joshua watched as Moses bore the weight of the people's rebellion. He saw the burden of leadership up close and realized that leadership wasn't just about power—it was about responsibility.

During those 40 years in the wilderness, Joshua served faithfully, even when it seemed thankless. He didn't seek glory or position; he focused on the mission. His commitment wasn't to Moses as a man—it was to the greater purpose of leading God's people to the Promised Land. Joshua's faithfulness in small tasks prepared him for greater challenges. When Moses passed away, God chose Joshua to lead the Israelites. The mantle of leadership wasn't thrust upon him by chance—it was earned through years of dedication, learning, and growth.

In the corporate world, I've seen people rush into leadership roles without understanding the demands of the position. They focus on authority but neglect the skills and character development that come from following. Inevitably, they stumble under the weight of expectations they weren't prepared for.

Then there are people like my friend Angela. Angela spent 15 years working under a demanding but brilliant CEO. She didn't always agree with him, but she studied his decision-making, absorbed his wisdom, and supported his vision. When the CEO retired, Angela was the natural choice to succeed him. Her followership had prepared her to lead.

Followership is not about passivity or blind obedience. It's about active engagement, learning, and contributing to a greater mission. In followership, you develop humility by recognizing that leadership is not about personal glory. You increase in empathy by understanding the challenges and pressures of leadership, and you gain resilience by persevering through difficult seasons, knowing they prepare you for what's ahead.

Joshua's years in the wilderness were not wasted—they were the foundation for his success.

HUMBLE INFLUENCE STORIES

Lisa's Corporate Odyssey – From Trainee to Trailblazer

Lisa, an ambitious MBA graduate, landed a coveted spot in a management trainee program at a global corporation. At first, she viewed the role as a stepping stone to the leadership position she craved. Instead of managing teams or leading projects, her responsibilities included shadowing department heads, attending meetings, and performing what she perceived as mundane tasks like compiling reports.

Lisa's frustration grew. She thought, *I didn't endure years of case studies and late-night group projects just to follow others around.* But her perspective began to shift after an informal lunch with one of the company's senior executives, Mr. Reed.

Mr. Reed recounted his journey, starting from an entry-level role in logistics. "Lisa," he said, "Leadership isn't just about making decisions—it's about making informed decisions. You can't guide others if you don't understand their work."

Taking his words to heart, Lisa started approaching her assignments with curiosity and purpose. She asked department heads questions about their challenges, observed their decision-making processes, and meticulously documented what worked and what didn't. In the marketing department, she learned how customer insights drive branding strategies. In operations, she saw the importance of efficiency and precision.

Three years later, Lisa was promoted to manage a struggling department. Drawing on her accumulated knowledge, she streamlined processes, fostered collaboration, and revitalized the team's morale. Within a year, the department's performance exceeded company expectations, earning Lisa recognition as a rising star.

Reflecting on her journey, she realized her time as a follower wasn't a detour—it was a masterclass in leadership.

Lisa's corporate odyssey underscores that followership is not a lesser role but an essential phase of preparation. Like Joshua under Moses, her willingness to learn, adapt, and serve laid the foundation for her leadership success.

Raj's Startup Apprenticeship – Building a Legacy

Raj, a software engineer with a passion for innovation, dreamed of launching his own tech startup. He envisioned disrupting industries, pitching to venture capitalists, and building cutting-edge solutions. However, he lacked a clear plan for navigating the challenges of running a business.

To prepare, Raj joined a mid-sized software firm as a product manager. He reported directly to an experienced CEO, Ms. Jackson, whose disciplined approach to decision-making often clashed with Raj's quick-moving, risk-taking personality. Ms. Jackson was meticulous, often insisting on rigorous market research and cost analysis before greenlighting projects.

At first, Raj found her methods stifling. He thought, *Why waste time overanalyzing when we could already be building?* But as he observed her leadership in action, he began to see the wisdom in her approach. During a major product rollout, Ms. Jackson faced a crisis when a critical feature malfunctioned during a demo with key clients. Instead of panicking, she calmly assessed the situation, redirected the team's focus, and salvaged the deal by pivoting to showcase other product strengths.

That moment stuck with Raj. He realized that leadership wasn't just about vision; it was about resilience, strategic thinking, and the ability to inspire confidence in the face of setbacks.

When Raj finally launched his startup, he found himself applying many of the principles he had learned under Ms. Jackson. He built a culture of data-driven decision-making, prioritized customer feedback, and fostered a sense of accountability within his team. Within five years, his startup became a market leader in its niche.

Raj's apprenticeship highlights the transformative power of followership. Much like Joshua observed Moses' leadership through triumphs and trials, Raj's time under Ms. Jackson equipped him to lead with confidence and clarity.

Maria's Nonprofit Journey – From Volunteer to Visionary

Maria's dream was to make a difference in the lives of underserved children through education. Inspired by her passion, she envisioned opening a nonprofit tutoring center. However, instead of diving headfirst into establishing her organization, Maria decided to spend time volunteering at a well-established education nonprofit in her city.

She started with small tasks: organizing book drives, tutoring students, and assisting with events. Over time, she took on more responsibilities, eventually coordinating a citywide literacy program. During these years, Maria worked closely with the nonprofit's executive director, Mr. Thompson. She watched him navigate the complexities of nonprofit management—balancing fundraising, donor relations, staff recruitment, and program execution.

Maria didn't always agree with Mr. Thompson's decisions. She thought his cautious approach to growth sometimes stifled the organization's potential. But rather than dismiss his methods, she sought to understand them. She realized that every move he made, whether conservative or bold, was grounded in the long-term sustainability of the nonprofit's mission.

When the time came for Maria to launch her tutoring center, she felt prepared for the challenges ahead. She implemented many of the strategies she had learned, from cultivating relationships with donors to creating measurable impact reports. Her center quickly became a beacon of hope in the community, attracting more students, volunteers, and funding than she had ever anticipated.

Maria often reflected on her time under Mr. Thompson's mentorship. "Those years weren't just about helping kids," she said. "They were about learning how to lead an organization with purpose."

Maria's story parallels Joshua's transformation from follower to leader. Her willingness to observe, learn, and serve under an experienced leader prepared her to make her vision a reality.

There are common threads in these stories. Each of these stories highlights key takeaways from Joshua's journey: *The Strength in Humility*- just as Joshua faithfully served Moses, these individuals embraced followership as an opportunity to grow, rather than a limitation, *The Power of Observation*- by observing seasoned leaders, they gained insights that would later inform their own leadership styles, and *The Value of Patience*- like Joshua's years in the wilderness, these periods of preparation shaped their resilience and readiness for leadership.

These real-world scenarios remind us that every leader's journey begins with a willingness to follow, learn, and grow. Following is not the opposite of leading—it's the foundation of it.

KEY TAKEAWAY

Joshua's story reminds us that leadership is not an instant destination—it's a journey that begins with faithful followership. By serving, learning, and growing, we prepare ourselves for the moments when we're called to lead.

So, if you find yourself in the role of a follower, take heart. You're not in the shadows—you're in the making.

"The LORD himself goes before you and will be with you; he will never leave you nor forsake you. Do not be afraid; do not be discouraged" —Deuteronomy 31:8

(This verse summarizes Joshua's preparation under Moses and the courage to step into leadership.)

REFLECTION

Think about your current role. Are you in a season of followership, preparing for something greater? Instead of rushing to lead, consider what you can learn in this season.
Ask yourself:
- How can I support my leader more effectively?
- What lessons can I take from their successes and failures?
- How can I align my efforts with the greater mission of my organization?

Your wilderness years, like Joshua's, may feel long and unglamorous. But they are shaping you into the person you're meant to become.

"He who cannot be a
good follower cannot be
a good leader."

–Aristotle

CHAPTER 2: THE LAW OF FOLLOWING

The Law of Followership: effective leadership is rooted in first mastering the art of followership, as it develops the humility, discipline, and insight necessary to lead others successfully.

In 1970, the Apollo 13 spacecraft faced an unforeseen and catastrophic explosion that threatened the lives of the three astronauts onboard. The situation was dire—oxygen supplies were running out, power systems were failing, and the journey back to Earth seemed impossible. The world remembers the steady and courageous leadership of Mission Commander Jim Lovell, who kept his crew calm and focused under extreme pressure. Yet, the true heroes of this story extended far beyond the spacecraft. The NASA engineers and technicians on the ground, armed with little more than slide rules and sheer ingenuity, demonstrated extraordinary followership in the face of insurmountable odds.

These unsung heroes worked tirelessly to devise life-saving solutions for the astronauts. With precision and creativity, they tested and recalibrated methods in real-time, solving complex problems with limited resources. Their unwavering commitment, adaptability, and critical thinking turned a potential tragedy into a triumphant rescue. The Apollo 13 mission stands as a powerful testament to the interdependence of leadership and followership. While Lovell's leadership provided direction and reassurance, it was the collective effort of the followers—the engineers and technicians—who brought his vision to life.

This story underscores an essential truth: the success of a leader depends on the effectiveness of their followers. Leadership often commands the spotlight, but followership drives the outcomes. A leader's vision remains an idea unless followers work together to make it a reality. It's like a conductor leading an orchestra. The conductor sets the tempo, cues the musicians, and interprets the score. But the beauty of the performance depends entirely on the skill and coordination of the musicians. Without their dedication and discipline, the conductor's efforts are meaningless.

Effective followership requires certain traits that transcend any specific role or field. Commitment to the mission is paramount— great followers believe in the leader's vision and align their efforts with the organization's goals, seeing their work as part of a greater purpose. Critical thinking ensures that followers contribute constructively, analyzing situations, identifying risks, and providing feedback to improve decision-making. Reliability is another cornerstone of effective followership, as leaders depend on their team to deliver results consistently, meet deadlines, and maintain high standards. Adaptability allows followers to adjust to changing circumstances without losing sight of the overarching mission. Finally, self-leadership sets great followers apart. They anticipate needs, solve problems, and take initiative without waiting for instructions.

By embracing the principles of followership, individuals elevate not only their leaders but their entire teams. Success becomes less about who gets the credit and more about achieving the mission together, exemplifying the transformative power of collective effort.

The Bible offers another powerful example of followership in the story of Aaron and Hur.

During a battle between the Israelites and the Amalekites, Moses stood on a hilltop, holding his staff above his head. As long as the staff was raised, the Israelites prevailed. But when Moses grew tired and lowered his hands, the Amalekites gained the upper hand. Seeing

Moses struggle, Aaron and Hur stepped in. They held his hands steady until sunset, ensuring the Israelites' victory.

Their actions were simple yet profound. They didn't try to take over or question Moses' leadership. Instead, they supported him in his moment of need, demonstrating that followership is not about submission—it's about partnership.

It is the followers who transform a leader's vision into reality, demonstrating that success is never a solo achievement but a collaborative effort. True followership is not about passive obedience; it's a dynamic partnership. Great followers actively engage, think critically, and take initiative, ensuring that the team remains aligned with its mission. Leadership may often stand in the spotlight, but the collective effort of dedicated followers is what makes true success possible.

Just as great followership enables success, poor followership can derail even the best leaders. Consider the corporate scandals of companies like Enron and Theranos. In these cases, leaders made disastrous decisions, but followers who might have raised concerns chose to stay silent. This lack of critical thinking and accountability among followers contributed to the companies' downfalls. Ineffective followership can manifest as *blind obedience*- failing to question flawed decisions, *complacency*- taking a passive role and waiting for others to act, or *resistance*- undermining leadership or fostering division. These behaviors not only harm organizations but also erode trust and morale.

To embody the law of following, these practices must be adopted: *align with the mission*- learn and understand the leader's vision and find ways to contribute meaningfully, *communicate proactively*- share updates, offer insights, and voice concerns constructively, *take ownership*-treat the team's goals as your own and take responsibility for your role in achieving them, *support your leader*- even when you disagree, work toward solutions that align with the greater good, and *celebrate collective success*- recognize that the team's achievements are more important than individual credit.

HUMBLE INFLUENCE STORIES

Karen's Story- A Deadline Missed

Karen was the project manager for a high-stakes product launch at a mid-sized tech company. Her team was a diverse mix of seasoned professionals and ambitious newcomers, each bringing unique strengths to the table. Together, they worked under Mark, the company's charismatic but occasionally disorganized executive. While Mark excelled in inspiring big-picture ideas, he often left the finer details and logistical challenges to his team—a reality that tested their resilience and problem-solving skills.

One week before the launch, disaster struck. A critical vendor failed to meet a major deadline, jeopardizing the entire project. The components needed for the final product assembly were delayed, and without immediate action, the launch would have to be postponed, potentially costing the company millions and damaging its reputation. *Communicate Proactively-* Karen called an emergency meeting, bringing her team together to assess the situation. Despite the high stakes, she remained calm, fostering an environment where everyone felt empowered to contribute.

The team demonstrated the principles of effective followership in action.

> *Took ownership-* rather than waiting for instructions or succumbing to frustration, they engaged in critical thinking. One member proposed reaching out to alternative vendors, while another suggested using existing resources to create a temporary workaround. Ideas flowed freely, each solution evaluated and refined collectively.

Supported their leader- their adaptability shone as they reorganized tasks, shifting focus to areas they could control while awaiting confirmation from new vendors. Timelines were adjusted, roles redistributed, and priorities reassigned—all without missing a beat. Commitment was the glue that held the team together.

Aligned with the mission- they worked late into the night, driven not by Mark's oversight but by their shared belief in the project's significance. For Karen's team, this wasn't just another product launch—it was an opportunity to showcase their skills and ensure the company's success. Their shared purpose transcended individual roles or recognition, motivating each member to give their all.

Celebrated collective success- on the day of the launch, the product went live without a hitch. Customers praised its seamless execution, and the company's leadership celebrated Mark's vision as the driving force behind the success. Mark received most of the credit, his name headlining press releases and company announcements. But Karen's team didn't mind. They knew that their collective effort, ingenuity, and unwavering dedication had made the impossible possible.

For them, the real reward wasn't recognition—it was the satisfaction of achieving the mission together, knowing they had exemplified the essence of great followership.

The Community Initiative – Aaron and Hur in Action

Emma was the founder of a grassroots organization dedicated to providing disaster relief to small communities, a mission close to her heart. When a hurricane devastated a coastal town, leaving homes flooded and families displaced, her team quickly mobilized. Donations poured in, volunteers stepped forward, and local authorities looked to Emma's organization to coordinate relief efforts. It was a massive operation, requiring around-the-clock focus and relentless determination.

At first, Emma worked tirelessly to manage the growing demands. She directed volunteers, coordinated supply chains, and liaised with local officials. But as the days wore on, the scale of the operation became overwhelming. Supplies were delayed, schedules clashed, and the community's needs grew with each passing hour. Emma, usually the unshakable leader, began to show signs of exhaustion. She was running on empty, caught between the critical details of the present and the strategic vision required for the long-term recovery effort.

Supported their leader- her two trusted deputy leaders, Carlos and Maya, recognized the strain Emma was under. Like modern-day Aaron and Hur, they stepped in to support her when she needed it most.

Aligned with the mission- their commitment to the mission was unwavering, but their approach was one of support, not usurpation.

Took ownership and communicated proactively- Carlos took over the logistics, streamlining the flow of supplies and ensuring that essentials like water and food were prioritized for the hardest-hit areas. He worked closely with transportation teams and local suppliers to eliminate bottlenecks, freeing Emma from the operational chaos. Maya, meanwhile, focused on volunteer management. She created clear, actionable schedules, resolved conflicts, and ensured every volunteer understood their role, transforming the once-chaotic work-force into a coordinated and effective team.

Carlos and Maya demonstrated exceptional self-leadership. They didn't wait for Emma to delegate tasks or tell them what needed to be done. Instead, they anticipated challenges and tackled them head-on. When a food shortage at one of the shelters threatened to escalate into a crisis, Carlos identified nearby resources and secured emergency shipments. Maya quickly reorganized the volunteer team to address the shortage without disrupting other critical operations. Their adaptability turned potential disasters into manageable problems, all while sparing Emma from further stress.

Celebrated collective success- by the end of the week, the operation had stabilized. Relief supplies were reaching those in need, volunteers were working in harmony, and the community began to see the light at the end of the tunnel. Emma, finally able to focus on the strategic aspects of recovery, thanked Carlos and Maya for their extraordinary efforts. Smiling, they reminded her, "We're here to hold up your hands when they're tired."

The story of Carlos and Maya mirrors the biblical account of Aaron and Hur supporting Moses as he grew weary during a battle. Their actions exemplify the power of effective followership—not as an attempt to overshadow leadership, but as a means of strengthening it. By taking initiative, adapting to challenges, and focusing on the collective mission, Carlos and Maya ensured Emma's leadership remained effective and the community's needs were met. This partnership highlights a fundamental truth: great followers don't seek to replace leaders—they empower them. Effective followership isn't about overshadowing leadership—it's about strengthening it through partnership and initiative.

The Crisis at ApolloTech – The Power of Unified Followership

ApolloTech, a leading technology company, was on the verge of launching a revolutionary software platform that promised to disrupt the industry. The stakes were high, with millions invested and shareholders expecting results. One week before launch, disaster struck: a critical bug in the software threatened to derail the project.

The team, led by Chief Technology Officer Sarah, faced immense pressure. But the real heroes of this story were the engineers and developers under Sarah's leadership, who embodied the principles of effective followership.

Aligned with the mission- every team member believed in the platform's potential. They weren't just working for a paycheck—they saw their contributions as pivotal to the company's future.

Communicated proactively- instead of succumbing to panic, they analyzed the problem. Developers brainstormed fixes, while quality assurance teams tested each solution in real-time.

Supported leadership- when the initial fixes failed, the team pivoted quickly, exploring alternative solutions while Sarah coordinated priorities.

Took ownership- no one waited for instructions. Each engineer took ownership of their role, solving smaller problems that, collectively, resolved the larger issue.

Celebrated collective success- the revolutionary software program launched successfully.

The team worked tirelessly for three straight days. Sarah's leadership provided direction, but it was the team's dedication and problem-solving skills that ensured the platform launched successfully. Like the NASA engineers during Apollo 13, the ApolloTech team demonstrated that effective followership can turn a potential disaster into a triumph. Their actions highlighted the interdependence of leadership and followership in achieving mission-critical goals.

The Orchestra of Success – Lessons from the Symphony

David, a young conductor, had just taken over a prestigious symphony orchestra. While he was excited to infuse his style into the group, he quickly realized that success depended less on his leadership and more on the musicians' followership.

During rehearsals for their debut performance, David introduced a bold interpretation of Beethoven's Ninth Symphony. It was unconventional, requiring the musicians to adjust their usual timing and dynamics. Initially, some resisted, questioning David's vision. Others simply went through the motions, failing to fully engage. Sensing the disconnect, David paused the rehearsal. He shared his passion for the piece, explaining how his interpretation captured the spirit of Beethoven's struggle and triumph. Slowly, the orchestra members began to align with his vision.

Alignment with the mission- the musicians embraced David's interpretation, recognizing that their work contributed to something greater than individual preferences.

Supported their leader- adjusting to the new style required them to unlearn habits and embrace a different approach.

Communicate proactively- the principal violinist and first clarinetist provided constructive feedback, helping David refine his cues to better guide the group.

Took ownership- each musician practiced diligently, ensuring their parts were flawless by performance night.

Celebrated collective success- performance earned a standing ovation.

When the curtain rose, the orchestra delivered a performance that earned a standing ovation. Critics praised not just David's bold interpretation but also the musicians' precision and passion. David's story illustrates how effective followership transforms a leader's vision into reality. Much like a conductor depends on musicians, leaders need followers who are committed, adaptable, and engaged.

KEY TAKEAWAY

The law of following reminds us that leadership and followership are two sides of the same coin. Success depends not just on the leader's vision but on the dedication, insight, and actions of those who follow.

Great leaders may get the credit, but great followers make the difference.

"Two are better than one, because they have a good return for their labor: If either of them falls down, one can help the other up" —Ecclesiastes 4:9-10

(This emphasizes the mutual strength found in followership and teamwork.)

REFLECTION

How are you supporting your leader? Are you aligned with your organization's mission?

Ask yourself:

- Am I proactively contributing to my team's success, or am I waiting for direction?
- Do I provide constructive feedback when I see risks or opportunities?
- How can I take more initiative to support the mission?

Effective followership is a choice. By embracing the law of following, you not only elevate your leader but also strengthen your team and your own potential for growth.

"The strength of the team is each individual member. The strength of each member is the team."

—Phil Jackson

CHAPTER 3: THE OFTEN OVERLOOKED POWER OF FOLLOWERS

During the 1960s, as NASA was immersed in its ambitious mission to land a man on the moon, President John F. Kennedy visited the space agency to see the work in progress. While touring the facility, he came across a janitor mopping the floor. Curious, Kennedy stopped and asked the man what he did at NASA. Without hesitation, the janitor looked up and replied, *"I'm helping put a man on the moon."*

At first glance, the janitor's job might seem inconsequential compared to the engineers designing rockets or the astronauts preparing for space travel. Yet, his response captured the essence of followership and the profound value of every role within an organization.

The janitor didn't see his work as merely cleaning floors—he saw it as a crucial piece of a much larger puzzle. By ensuring the facility was clean and functional, he supported the scientists and technicians who depended on a safe and efficient workspace to achieve their groundbreaking mission. His perspective was a testament to understanding the bigger picture, aligning personal effort with a collective goal.

This story underscores an important truth: no contribution is too small when it serves a greater purpose. The janitor's sense of purpose transformed what many might dismiss as a mundane task into a vital contribution to one of humanity's greatest achievements. He recognized that his work mattered, and that the success of the mission depended on the coordinated efforts of every individual, from the astronauts and engineers to the administrative staff and janitorial team. This perspective embodies the humility and dedication that define great followership.

Moreover, the janitor's response reveals a mindset that is rare and invaluable in any organization: the ability to connect one's daily tasks to the overarching vision. Such alignment not only fosters a sense of pride and purpose but also inspires others. His reply to President Kennedy was not just an expression of his role but a declaration of shared ownership in NASA's mission. It was a reminder that even the smallest acts, performed with intention and excellence, contribute to monumental outcomes.

Whether in a corporation, a nonprofit, or a community project, the success of a leader's vision depends on followers who understand the importance of their roles. Just as a rocket cannot launch without each bolt and circuit functioning perfectly, an organization cannot succeed without individuals who bring their best, regardless of title or task. The janitor at NASA didn't just clean floors—he exemplified the power of purpose-driven work and the profound impact of every contribution, no matter how seemingly small, on achieving something extraordinary.

Followers are the often-overlooked engine behind any successful endeavor. While leaders set the vision, it is followers who execute it, turning strategy into action, offering critical feedback, and fostering collaboration within teams. The strength of an organization lies not solely in its leadership but in the invaluable contributions of its followers.

A general needs soldiers to carry out battle plans. A conductor relies on musicians to bring a symphony to life. A CEO depends on employees to implement a company's vision. Without followers, leadership is like a ship without a crew—it may have direction, but it lacks the power to move forward.

Great followers possess unique qualities that not only support leaders but elevate the entire organization. *Commitment to the mission* is paramount. These followers do more than complete tasks—they are deeply aligned with the organization's purpose, understanding how their efforts contribute to the bigger picture. For example, during the early days of SpaceX, engineers worked tirelessly, driven by the mission to revolutionize space exploration. Their unwavering dedication turned Elon Musk's ambitious vision into a reality, proving that passion and alignment are essential to success.

Critical thinking is another hallmark of great followers. They question decisions when necessary, offering constructive feedback that strengthens outcomes. In the biblical story of Abigail, she demonstrated this quality when she intervened to prevent King David from attacking her household. Her wisdom not only averted disaster but earned David's respect, showcasing how thoughtful intervention can benefit both leaders and missions. Similarly, *reliability* is an indispensable trait. Leaders need followers they can count on to meet deadlines, deliver high-quality work, and uphold their commitments.

Adaptability is just as crucial. In a world where change is constant, great followers know how to pivot when circumstances shift, maintaining their focus on the mission even when the path to achieving it changes. They also excel in fostering *collaboration*, building trust and supporting peers to create a culture where everyone thrives. By working together, they amplify the team's collective strength.

The relationship between leaders and followers is not a one-way street—it is a reciprocal partnership. Effective followers empower their leaders by providing support, insights, and ideas. They drive the team forward by contributing to collective goals and influencing the organization with innovative solutions. In turn, leaders who value their followers create an environment where this partnership flourishes. They delegate meaningful responsibilities, provide mentorship and guidance, and recognize and celebrate their contributions.

When leaders and followers work together as partners, they create a powerful synergy that drives success. The interplay between vision and execution, direction and collaboration, creates a dynamic that ensures the mission not only survives but thrives. This partnership is the foundation of every great accomplishment.

Organizations that overlook the importance of followership risk: *reduced collaboration-* a lack of strong followers leads to silos and disjointed efforts, *poor decision-making-* without critical feedback, leaders may make flawed choices and *low morale-* when followers feel undervalued, their motivation and productivity decline. Effective followership is not about subordination—it's about contribution. Great followers don't merely execute tasks; they elevate their teams and leaders by bringing their unique strengths, perspectives, and initiative to the table.

The unique qualities of followers bring profound value to organizations. Their *commitment drives impact-* great followers are deeply invested in the mission, going beyond their job descriptions to contribute meaningfully. Their *critical thinking strengthens decisions-* by offering feedback, analyzing risks, and proposing solutions, effective followers enhance their leaders' decision-making. Their *reliability builds trust-* dependable followers create stability, ensuring that leaders and teams can rely on them in critical moments. Their *adaptability fuels resilience-* the ability to pivot and innovate during challenges enables teams to navigate uncertainty and achieve success. And their *collaboration creates synergy-* followers who foster trust and teamwork amplify the collective strength of their organizations.

As Phil Jackson's quote reminds us, "The strength of the team is each individual member. The strength of each member is the team." Followers and leaders alike share the responsibility for achieving success, proving that every role—no matter how small—matters in the pursuit of a common goal.

HUMBLE INFLUENCE STORIES

Karen's Hidden Leadership – Driving Success Behind the Scenes

Karen, a mid-level project manager at a tech company, had developed a reputation for reliability and precision. She wasn't the loudest voice in the room, nor did she seek attention. Her value to the organization became apparent during a high-stakes product launch that would either cement the company's reputation or jeopardize it entirely.

The project was led by Steve, a visionary CEO known for his bold ideas and unrelenting pace. However, his tendency to micromanage and overlook details often created challenges for his team. As the launch date approached, a series of vendor delays and technical issues threatened to derail the project.

Karen stepped in with the qualities of an exceptional follower:

Commitment to the mission- Karen was deeply aligned with the project's goals. She didn't just see her role as coordinating tasks; she viewed herself as a critical link in ensuring the launch's success.

Critical thinking- when the vendor delays surfaced, Karen didn't wait for Steve to solve the problem. She identified alternative suppliers, analyzed their capabilities, and presented solutions that minimized the disruptions.

Reliability- the team trusted Karen to foresee problems before they escalated. She created contingency plans, streamlined workflows, and ensured no task fell through the cracks.

Collaboration- Karen built strong relationships with her peers and external partners, fostering a spirit of cooperation even under pressure.

When the product launched successfully, Steve was celebrated as a bold leader. But Karen's team knew the truth, her quiet dedication and problem-solving turned his vision into reality. Karen exemplified being the backbone of the team's success, even when the spotlight shined elsewhere. Like NASA's janitor who helped "put a man on the moon," Karen's contributions proved that no role is too small to make a difference.

The SpaceX Engineers – Fueling Innovation Through Followership

During the early years of SpaceX, Elon Musk's vision to make space exploration affordable and sustainable seemed like an impossible dream. Skeptics doubted the viability of launching reusable rockets, citing the complexity and cost of such an endeavor. Yet, behind Musk's bold leadership stood a team of engineers and scientists who embodied the principles of great followership.

Commitment to the mission- SpaceX's engineers weren't just employees—they were believers in the mission to revolutionize space travel. They worked tirelessly, often pulling 80-hour weeks, driven by the shared purpose of achieving the impossible.

Critical thinking- instead of blindly following Musk's directives, the team constantly questioned assumptions, experimented with new approaches, and challenged each other to refine their methods. This culture of critical thinking was instrumental in solving complex technical problems.

Adaptability- the road to reusable rockets was paved with failures. Each explosion during testing was met with resilience, as the team quickly adapted, learned, and improved.

Self-leadership- SpaceX's engineers didn't wait for Musk to micromanage every aspect of their work. They took initiative, proposed solutions, and innovated relentlessly.

Their efforts culminated in the historic 2015 launch of the Falcon 9 rocket, the first reusable rocket to successfully land after reaching orbit. This achievement transformed the aerospace industry and validated Musk's vision. The SpaceX story highlights that while visionary leadership can inspire, it is the dedication and ingenuity of followers that make the vision a reality. Effective followers don't just support their leader—they actively drive progress.

The Healthcare Crisis – Collaboration Under Pressure

Dr. Emily, a newly appointed hospital director, faced an unprecedented challenge when her facility was hit by a sudden surge of patients during a viral outbreak. The situation was chaotic, with limited resources, overworked staff, and an overwhelmed emergency room. While Dr. Emily provided direction and made critical decisions, the real heroes were the nurses, technicians, and administrative staff who stepped up as effective followers.

Commitment to the mission- the staff didn't just see their roles as jobs; they understood the gravity of the situation and worked tirelessly to provide the best care possible. Many volunteered for extra shifts, driven by their dedication to patient welfare.

Collaboration- their teamwork became the cornerstone of success. Nurses collaborated with technicians to streamline triage procedures, while administrative staff coordinated supply deliveries and managed patient intake efficiently.

Critical thinking- amid the crisis, one nurse suggested reorganizing the triage area to prioritize high-risk patients more effectively. Her initiative improved patient outcomes and reduced wait times.

Adaptability- as new challenges arose—such as a shortage of ventilators—the staff quickly adapted. They implemented innovative solutions, including repurposing existing equipment to meet patient needs.

When the crisis subsided, the hospital's success was attributed to Dr. Emily's leadership. But she was quick to point out that her role was made possible by the unwavering dedication and ingenuity of her team.This underscores the importance of the reciprocal relationship between leaders and followers. Dr. Emily's team demonstrated that effective followership is not passive—it is proactive, collaborative, and essential to achieving success under pressure.

KEY TAKEAWAY

Followers are not just cogs in a machine—they are the driving force behind success. By embracing the principles of effective followership, you can elevate your contributions, strengthen your team, and create a lasting impact.

In the next chapter, we'll explore the importance of understanding your "why" and how it fuels purpose and performance in followership.

"Do nothing out of selfish ambition or vain conceit. Rather, in humility value others above yourselves, not looking to your own interests"
—Philippians 2:3-4

(This captures the humility and value that effective followers bring to a team.)

REFLECTION

Take a moment to evaluate your role as a follower.
- What strengths do you bring to your team?
- How do your actions contribute to your organization's mission?
- Are there areas where you can grow or add more value?

By focusing on your value as a follower, you not only support your leader and team but also position yourself for growth and future opportunities.

"Efforts and courage
are not enough without
purpose and direction."

—John F. Kennedy

CHAPTER 4: UNDERSTANDING THE WHY

It was a crisp autumn morning when I met Leah, a talented software developer at a growing tech firm. She had all the qualities of an effective follower—reliable, adaptable, and innovative. Yet, over coffee, she admitted feeling stuck.

"I just don't see the point anymore," Leah said, staring into her mug. "I'm doing the work, but it's like I've lost my sense of purpose."

Her frustration wasn't uncommon. Many people, no matter how skilled or driven, face moments when their work feels disconnected from their deeper motivations. That's when understanding your "why" becomes essential.

Finding your "why" requires a deep sense of introspection and intentionality. It begins with reflecting on the moments when you've felt the most fulfilled in your work. Think back to times when you were truly energized and passionate about what you were doing. What activities brought you joy? Who were you helping? For Leah, a software developer, the answer came when she realized that her fulfillment didn't just come from writing code—it came from solving problems that improved people's lives. Her "why" wasn't just about the technical aspects of her job; it was about creating tools that made tasks easier and lives better for others.

Understanding your values is another essential step in uncovering your purpose. Your values act as a compass, guiding your decisions and actions. When you align your work with these core principles, you create a sense of harmony and meaning. Take time to write down your top three values and reflect on how your current role embodies—or could embody—those values. For instance, if creativity, integrity, and collaboration are central to your identity, how does your daily work reflect those ideals? If there's a gap, consider ways to bridge it.

Purpose often comes into focus when you consider the impact of your work. Ask yourself: Who benefits from what I do? Understanding the ripple effects of your efforts can be incredibly motivating. For a teacher, the "why" might be found in watching students grow and achieve their potential. For a designer, it might be in creating products or spaces that are both beautiful and functional. Recognizing the people or causes that your work touches can provide clarity and inspiration.

If you're struggling to connect with your role, it can help to revisit your organization's mission. Understanding how your work contributes to the broader goals of your company or team can reinforce your sense of purpose. Even tasks that feel routine or disconnected may play a vital role in advancing the bigger picture. Finding alignment between your efforts and the mission of your organization can reinvigorate your sense of belonging and significance.

Discovering your "why" is not a one-time task but an ongoing process of reflection, connection, and growth. By examining what drives you, understanding your values, considering your impact, and aligning with a greater mission, you can uncover a deeper sense of purpose in both your work and your life.

Nehemiah was a cupbearer to the king of Persia—a trusted but humble position. Yet when he heard about the ruined walls of Jerusalem, he felt a deep sense of purpose.Nehemiah didn't aspire to lead, but his "why" drove him to act. With the king's blessing, he returned to Jerusalem, rallied the people, and oversaw the rebuilding of the city's walls. His work wasn't about personal glory; it was about restoring his community. Nehemiah's story reminds us that purpose, not position, is what drives true impact.

Simon Sinek popularized the idea of starting with "why," but it's not a new concept. Purpose has always been a driving force for human achievement. Purpose provides clarity, energy, and resilience. It reminds us why our work matters and how it contributes to something greater than ourselves. For followers, knowing your "why" transforms your role from a series of tasks into a meaningful journey.

There are benefits of knowing your "why". It brings clarity to your purpose which helps you focus on what truly matters, cutting through the distractions and uncertainty. It gives motivation, when driven by your why even challenging tasks feel worthwhile. You can gain resilience, your purpose anchors you during difficult times, giving you the strength to persevere. And it brings fulfillment, knowing your why transforms work from a chore into a source of joy and meaning.

At the heart of discovering your why and purpose is curiosity—a willingness to explore, ask deeper questions, and seek new perspectives. When you cultivate the trait of curiosity, you move beyond routine tasks and start to see the bigger picture of your work. Curiosity is what prompts us to ask: *Why does this work matter? How does my role contribute to something greater? What else could I be learning or doing to expand my impact?*

Curiosity doesn't just help individuals find their purpose; it fuels innovation, deepens relationships, and strengthens followership. Those who ask questions, seek feedback, and explore new perspectives don't just follow orders—they shape the direction of their teams and organizations.

Esther, a young Jewish woman, became queen of Persia. When her people faced extermination, her cousin Mordecai reminded her of her purpose: "Who knows whether you have come to the kingdom for such a time as this?" With her "why" clear, Esther risked her life to advocate for her people, saving them from destruction. Her story illustrates how understanding your purpose empowers you to act with courage and conviction.

Not everyone finds their "why" immediately. Sometimes, purpose feels distant or unclear. That's okay. Here's how to reconnect: Experiment- take on new challenges or projects. Purpose often emerges when we step outside our comfort zones. Seek Feedback- ask colleagues or mentors what they see as your strengths. Their perspective can provide valuable insights into your "why." And be patient- purpose evolves over time. What drives you today might look different in the future. Stay open to growth and change.

HUMBLE INFLUENCE STORIES

Leah's Awakening – From Coding to Creating Impact

Leah, a skilled software developer, felt stuck. Her workdays were filled with debugging, writing code, and attending meetings, but something was missing. Over coffee one morning, she confessed, "I don't know why I'm doing this anymore. I know I'm good at what I do, but it feels so... meaningless."

Her company's mission was clear: build user-friendly tech solutions for small businesses. Yet Leah struggled to see how her efforts contributed to that vision. Her manager, Alex, noticed her disengagement and invited her to join a client feedback session.

During the session, Leah listened as a small bakery owner described how the company's software helped streamline operations and save hours each week. The owner said, "Your product has given me back time with my kids. I can't thank you enough."

Hearing those words lit a spark in Leah. She realized her "why" wasn't just coding—it was creating tools that made life easier for others. With her purpose reignited, Leah became more engaged and innovative, proposing features that enhanced the software's usability.

Simon Sinek once said, "Working hard for something we don't care about is called stress. Working hard for something we love is called passion." Leah's rediscovery of her "why" transformed her work into a source of passion and fulfillment. Understanding your "why" connects your daily tasks to a greater purpose, fueling motivation and creativity.

The Small Business That Found Its Purpose

Jay owned a small graphic design agency. His team created logos, brochures, and websites for various clients, but they often felt like they were spinning their wheels. The work paid the bills, but Jay noticed his team lacked enthusiasm and struggled to see the impact of their work.

One day, Jay attended a workshop on Simon Sinek's "Start with Why." Inspired, he gathered his team and posed a simple question: "Why do we do what we do?" At first, the answers were generic— "to make money," "to deliver good designs," "to meet client needs." Then one designer, Mia, shared a story about how a logo they created helped a local nonprofit gain more visibility and increase donations.

"That's why I love this work," Mia said. "We help people tell their stories and make a difference."

Jay and his team realized their "why" wasn't just about creating designs; it was about empowering clients to achieve their goals and tell their unique stories. With this clarity, Jay rebranded the agency with the tagline: "Designing Futures, One Story at a Time."

The shift in purpose energized the team. They began seeking out clients who aligned with their values—nonprofits, small businesses, and entrepreneurs with meaningful missions. Their work became more intentional, and their clients noticed the difference. For small businesses, discovering the "why" can align the team, attract like-minded clients, and transform work into a meaningful mission.

Nehemiah's Mission – Purpose in Action

The story of Nehemiah is one of the most compelling examples of purpose-driven followership in the Bible. As a cupbearer to King Artaxerxes of Persia, Nehemiah held a trusted but modest position, far removed from the corridors of real power. Yet, when he learned of the ruined walls of Jerusalem and the suffering of his people, he experienced a profound calling to act. His role as a cupbearer may not have been one of influence, but it was rooted in trust, reliability, and proximity to the king—qualities that became critical as he pursued his mission.

Nehemiah's first act of followership was his bold approach to the king. He sought permission to leave his post, resources to fund the rebuilding of Jerusalem's walls, and letters of safe passage to ensure his journey would succeed. This was no small request. It required courage, wisdom, and faith in God's purpose. Nehemiah didn't try to usurp authority or act independently; instead, he worked within the framework of his role, aligning his personal mission with the king's approval and support. His ability to follow the proper channels while passionately pursuing his vision underscores the balance between humility and initiative that defines great followership.

Upon arriving in Jerusalem, Nehemiah transitioned from a follower of the king to a servant-leader of the people. He surveyed the broken walls, assessed the extent of the damage, and rallied the people to the task. His leadership was inspiring, but it was also rooted in his ability to follow the will of God and the needs of the community. Nehemiah understood that rebuilding the walls required more than just a plan—it demanded the collective effort and dedication of an entire city. He mobilized priests, nobles, and commoners alike, assigning each group specific sections of the wall to rebuild. Families worked side by side, motivated not by personal gain but by a shared purpose: to restore their city and protect their people.

Nehemiah's story also highlights the challenges of follower-ship. As the rebuilding progressed, opposition arose. External enemies mocked their efforts and threatened violence, attempting to intimidate the workers into abandoning the mission. Internally, the people faced fatigue and discouragement as they grappled with the enormity of the task. Nehemiah's response was a masterclass in collaborative leadership and followership. He armed the workers, encouraged them to stay vigilant, and reminded them of the significance of their work. His rallying cry in Nehemiah 4:14, "Do not be afraid. Remember the Lord, who is great and awesome, and fight for your families, your sons and your daughters, your wives and your homes," reignited their determination.

Ultimately, the walls were rebuilt in an astonishing 52 days—a feat that would not have been possible without the collective dedication of the people and their willingness to follow Nehemiah's guidance. His success was not the result of his position or title but of his ability to inspire, organize, and align the community around a common goal. Nehemiah's role as a follower of the king and a follower of God's calling allowed him to lead effectively, demonstrating that followership is not about subordination but about purpose, partnership, and perseverance.

This account underscores a vital truth: great followership is not passive. It involves courage, initiative, and a willingness to serve a purpose greater than oneself. Nehemiah's story shows how effective followers can transform a vision into reality, overcoming obstacles through faith, collaboration, and unwavering commitment. In rebuilding Jerusalem's walls, Nehemiah left a legacy of what it means to be a purpose-driven follower and a servant-leader. Nehemiah's story illustrates that understanding your "why" empowers you to overcome obstacles and inspire others to join in achieving a shared goal.

Finding your "why" transforms work from a series of tasks into a meaningful mission. Understanding your purpose provides clarity, motivation, and resilience.

As Simon Sinek reminds us: "People don't buy what you do; they buy why you do it." When you connect with your purpose, you inspire not just yourself but those around you, creating a ripple effect of impact and fulfillment.

In your journey, remember that purpose is not static—it evolves. Stay curious, reflect often, and let your "why" guide your work, ensuring that every effort contributes to something greater than yourself.

KEY TAKEAWAY

Understanding your "why" transforms your role from a series of tasks into a mission. It connects your efforts to a greater purpose, bringing clarity, motivation, and fulfillment to your work.

In the next chapter, we'll explore how breaking the myth that followership is "easy" can unlock your potential as an active, engaged contributor.

"And we know that in all things God works for the good of those who love him, who have been called according to his purpose" —Romans 8:28

(This reflects the importance of aligning with a higher purpose.)

REFLECTION

Take a moment to reflect on your role:
- What excites you about your work?
- Who benefits from what you do?
- How does your role align with your values?

Your "why" is your anchor. It keeps you grounded in the face of challenges and guides your contributions toward something meaningful.

*Exercises to Find Your Why in Additional Resources at the end of the book

"Success is no accident.
It is hard work,
perseverance, learning,
studying, sacrifice, and
most of all, love of what
you are doing."

—Pelé

CHAPTER 5: BREAKING THE MYTH OF INTUITIVE FOLLOWERSHIP

The Myth of Intuitive Followership is the mistaken belief that effective followership comes naturally or requires no deliberate effort, training, or skill development. It assumes that simply being in a subordinate role is enough to fulfill the responsibilities of a follower and that following well is instinctive, rather than an intentional practice.

I once worked with a young marketing associate named Claire who had just joined a nonprofit organization. She was bright, eager, and full of enthusiasm, but her understanding of followership was, well, simplistic.

"All I have to do is follow instructions, right?" she said one afternoon, a little smile tugging at the corners of her mouth.

It wasn't long before Claire realized that followership was far from easy. During a major fundraising campaign, her manager fell ill just weeks before the event. Without clear instructions, Claire felt overwhelmed. Tasks were piling up, decisions needed to be made, and team members were looking to her for guidance.

Claire could have waited for direction or hoped someone else would take the lead. Instead, she stepped up. She clarified the team's goals, reorganized tasks, and kept everyone aligned. The event not only went off without a hitch—it exceeded expectations.

That experience taught Claire, and the rest of us watching, a vital lesson: *followership is not passive. It's an active, intentional process that requires initiative, critical thinking, and problem-solving.*

Many people mistakenly assume that followership is simple—a matter of carrying out orders and staying in the background. It's often seen as the easier counterpart to leadership, requiring little effort or thought. But this couldn't be further from the truth. Effective followership is a skill that demands deliberate effort, reflection, and practice. Just as great leaders are not born but developed, great followers must cultivate the abilities that allow them to excel in their roles.

One common misconception is that *followership is passive.* This mindset imagines followers as people who merely execute tasks, obey commands, and avoid making waves. But true followership is far from passive. Great followers actively engage with their leaders, offering feedback, sharing insights, and taking initiative to advance the mission. They understand the vision of their leaders and work to align their efforts in ways that drive success, often anticipating challenges and proposing solutions before being asked. Far from being passive participants, effective followers are dynamic contributors.

Another myth is that *followership is easy.* Leadership may appear more challenging because it carries visible responsibility and often faces public scrutiny, but followership requires its own set of nuanced and demanding skills. Effective followers must navigate complex relationships, balancing loyalty to their leaders with the courage to offer constructive criticism when needed. They must maintain accountability to both their team and the mission while finding ways to contribute meaningfully to shared goals. These skills—often invisible to outsiders—are as critical to the success of any organization as the leadership itself.

Followership is not a fallback for those who do not aspire to lead; it is an essential, active role that demands discipline, insight, and a commitment to the greater good. Those who excel at followership recognize its challenges and embrace its complexities, knowing that their contributions are just as vital to the success of the mission as those of the leaders they support.

The story of Ruth in the Bible illustrates the depth and intentionality of effective followership. After her husband's death, Ruth chose to follow her mother-in-law, Naomi, back to Bethlehem, despite having no obligation to do so. Her words to Naomi resonate deeply: "Where you go, I will go, and where you stay, I will stay. Your people will be my people and your God my God."

Ruth didn't follow passively. She worked tirelessly to support Naomi, gleaning fields to provide for them both. Her loyalty and initiative not only ensured their survival but also led to a new chapter in her life as the great-grandmother of King David. Ruth's story reminds us that followership is about commitment, resilience, and the willingness to take action.

Many people default to passive followership, allowing leaders to make decisions and steer the course without much input. But why is this the case? Several barriers often prevent individuals from embracing active followership, each rooted in hesitation, doubt, or organizational culture.

One common barrier is the *fear of overstepping*. Followers may hesitate to speak up or take initiative, worrying that their actions might be perceived as challenging authority or undermining their leader. This fear can create a dynamic where followers hold back, even when they have valuable insights or ideas to offer. Overcoming this requires building trust with your leader. Approaching feedback or suggestions with respect and positive intent helps establish a collaborative relationship, where contributions are seen as support rather than confrontation.

Another barrier is a *lack of confidence*. Many followers doubt their ability to add value or make impactful decisions, believing that their role is to simply execute tasks without question. This mindset can stifle their potential and limit their contributions. The key to overcoming this is to start small—take ownership of a single task or project. By successfully managing smaller responsibilities, followers can gradually build their confidence and demonstrate their ability to lead from within.

Cultural norms within organizations can also discourage active followership. In environments with rigid hierarchies or authoritarian leadership styles, followers may feel constrained by unwritten rules that discourage stepping outside traditional roles. However, even in such settings, opportunities exist to contribute meaningfully within one's sphere of influence. Small, subtle actions—like offering thoughtful solutions during meetings or proactively addressing minor challenges—can foster a culture of collaboration and show that followership is not about undermining authority but about supporting shared goals.

Active followership is not about replacing leadership; it's about enhancing it. By recognizing and overcoming these barriers, followers can move beyond passive roles to become dynamic, engaged participants in their organizations, contributing value in ways that strengthen both leaders and teams.

HUMBLE INFLUENCE STORIES

Claire's Growth – From Passive to Proactive

Claire, a marketing associate, began her nonprofit career with enthusiasm but little understanding of the complexities of followership. Early on, she believed her role was simply to follow instructions from her manager. However, when her manager fell ill just weeks before a major fundraising event, Claire was thrust into a position where passive followership was no longer an option.

Initially overwhelmed, Claire took a moment to reassess her approach. She realized the team needed clarity, direction, and a unified focus. Drawing on her knowledge of the campaign's goals, Claire stepped up:

Initiative- she gathered input from her team to identify gaps and immediate needs.

Critical thinking- she prioritized tasks, delegated responsibilities, and streamlined workflows.

Problem-solving- rather than waiting for further direction, she took ownership of unresolved issues, including negotiating with vendors and finalizing event logistics.

The event exceeded expectations, raising 30 percent more than projected. Claire's team credited her decisive actions and ability to lead from the middle, while Claire realized that effective followership is far from passive—it's about active engagement and stepping up when needed.

Simon Sinek's quote, "Leadership is not about being in charge. It is about taking care of those in your charge," captures the essence of Claire's transformation. By focusing on her team's needs and the mission's success, Claire proved that proactive followership can make all the difference.

The Small Business Shift – A Bakery's Turnaround

When Melissa took over her family bakery, she inherited a loyal but passive team accustomed to simply following orders. The bakery was struggling; sales were stagnant, and customer engagement was low.

Melissa knew that to revive the business, she needed her team to adopt a more proactive approach. She started by holding a meeting to discuss their shared vision. "This isn't just about baking bread," she said. "It's about creating a place where people feel welcome, cared for, and connected." Inspired, her employees began to step up:

Critical-thinking- Melissa introduced a customer loyalty program, her team embraced the change and brainstormed creative ways to promote it.

Initiative- one employee, Raj, suggested introducing a weekly "community bake night," where customers could learn baking skills. The idea became a hit, boosting sales and community engagement.

Problem-solving- the team started working together more cohesively, sharing ideas to improve efficiency and enhance the customer experience.

Within six months, the bakery's revenue increased by 40 percent. The team's shift from passive to active followership not only saved the business but also created a thriving workplace culture. Like Melissa's team, small businesses thrive when employees embrace active followership. By taking initiative and aligning their actions with the larger mission, they contribute to a collective success that extends beyond their individual roles.

The Ruth Principle – Loyalty and Action in Crisis

The biblical story of Ruth offers a timeless example of breaking the myth of intuitive followership. After her husband's death, Ruth faced a crossroads: return to her family or follow her mother-in-law, Naomi, back to Bethlehem. Ruth chose the latter, not out of obligation but from a deep sense of loyalty and purpose.

Ruth's commitment went beyond words. She worked tirelessly to provide for Naomi, gleaning fields under harsh conditions and navigating the uncertainties of life in a new land. Her actions reflected key traits of active, intentional followership:

Initiative- despite personal loss and challenges, Ruth remained focused on supporting Naomi.

Problem-solving- she took proactive steps to secure their survival, seeking out opportunities to gather food and resources.

Critical-thinking- Ruth adjusted to a new environment, embracing unfamiliar customs and earning the trust of those around her.

Ruth's efforts ultimately led to her marriage to Boaz and a place in the lineage of King David. Her story reminds us that followership is not passive submission—it is a dynamic combination of loyalty, resilience, and action. Ruth's journey illustrates that even in roles of followership, taking initiative and acting with purpose can lead to profound impact and transformation.

Simon Sinek's insight, "The role of a leader is not to come up with all the great ideas. The role of a leader is to create an environment in which great ideas can happen," underscores the value of active followership. Leaders succeed when followers engage proactively, driving progress through their own contributions. By breaking the myth of intuitive followership, individuals unlock their potential, strengthening teams and creating lasting impact in their organizations and communities.

KEY TAKEAWAY

Followership isn't just about doing what you're told—it's about actively and intentionally contributing through initiative, critical-thinking and problem-solving. By cultivating the skills of active followership, you can transform your role and unlock your potential.

In the next chapter, we'll explore the importance of building strong connections with your leader and team, diving into the strategies that foster trust, collaboration, and mutual respect.

"Instruct the wise and they will be wiser still; teach the righteous and they will add to their learning" —Proverbs 9:9

(Effective followership requires intentional learning and skill development.)

REFLECTION

Ask yourself:
- Do I wait for direction, or do I take initiative?
- How often do I provide constructive feedback to my leader or team?
- In what ways can I grow as an engaged, proactive contributor?

Breaking the myth of intuitive followership means stepping into your role with purpose and intention. It's about recognizing that followership is not passive—it's an active, intentional force that shapes success.

"The most important thing in communication is hearing what isn't said."

—Peter Drucker

CHAPTER 6: MANY COMMUNICATE – FEW CONNECT

In my first management role, I was assigned to lead a cross-functional team at an established, yet growing organization. While I was eager to prove myself as a leader, I quickly realized that my success depended on something more profound than strategy or technical expertise—it depended on *connection*.

My ability to lead was directly tied to the relationships I built with my team members. And as I learned later, the same principle applies to followership: strong connections between leaders and followers are the foundation of trust, collaboration, and success. Connection goes beyond surface-level rapport; it's about fostering relationships that enable open communication, mutual respect, and shared goals. When followers establish meaningful connections with their leaders, the entire team benefits from a stronger foundation of trust and collaboration.

At its core, connection fosters trust, the indispensable currency of leadership and followership. When leaders and followers trust one another, they create an environment of mutual confidence in each other's intentions and abilities. This trust lays the groundwork for teams to take risks, share ideas, and work together without fear of judgment or failure. Connection also enhances communication. Clear and open exchanges between leaders and followers reduce misunderstandings, ensure alignment on goals, and promote transparency. When team members feel comfortable sharing their thoughts and feedback, it paves the way for stronger decision-making and a more cohesive approach to challenges.

Collaboration naturally strengthens in a culture of connection. Followers who feel genuinely connected to their leaders and peers are more likely to contribute their skills and ideas toward shared goals. This sense of belonging and mutual respect fosters teamwork and amplifies the collective potential of the group. Beyond practical benefits, connection also boosts morale. When relationships are built on respect and empathy, they create a positive team culture where individuals feel valued and engaged. This sense of positivity improves overall morale, making teams not only more effective but also more resilient in the face of challenges.

Strong connections within teams are about more than just working together—they are about thriving together. Leaders and followers who prioritize meaningful relationships create an environment where trust, communication, collaboration, and morale flourish, driving success for everyone involved.

One of the greatest examples of connection in leadership and followership comes from Jesus and His disciples. Jesus didn't just teach His disciples—He built deep, personal relationships with them. He shared meals, listened to their concerns, and encouraged them. This connection created a bond of trust that inspired the disciples to follow Him wholeheartedly, even in the face of persecution. To be clear: Jesus' connection with His followers was about authority. However, His connection was based on love, respect, and shared purpose.

In Matthew 28:16-20, Jesus establishes His ultimate authority, declaring that "all authority in heaven and on earth"has been given to Him. As the perfect leader, He commands His disciples to carry out His mission, entrusting them with the Great Commission to "go and make disciples of all nations."

The disciples, though once uncertain and fearful, demonstrate great followership by obeying His command, worshiping Him, and committing to spreading His teachings. Their willingness to follow, despite their doubts, shows their faith, humility, and dedication to Jesus' mission. Through their obedience, they became not only devoted followers but also leaders who carried His message to the world, fulfilling His promise to be with them "always, to the very end of the age."

Connection happens when we *practice empathy*- empathy is the cornerstone of connection. Take time to understand your leader- their goals, challenges, and motivations, *communicate proactively*- don't wait for your leader to reach out—initiate conversations. Keep them informed of your progress, share ideas, and ask for feedback, *find common ground*- look for shared interests or values that can strengthen your bond. Whether it's a shared commitment to the organization's mission or a mutual hobby, commonalities build trust, *show consistency*- be reliable and consistent in your actions. Trust is built over time through dependability, and *invest in the relationship*- building connection takes effort. Show genuine interest in your leader's perspective and make time for meaningful interactions.

While connection is vital, it must be balanced with professionalism. Here's how to maintain this balance: *Respect boundaries*- avoid becoming overly personal or informal, especially in workplace settings, *focus on the mission*- keep your relationship grounded in the organization's goals and shared purpose and *communicate expectations*- be clear about your own boundaries and respect those of your leader.

Despite its importance, building connections can be challenging. Common barriers include: *hierarchical distance*- a rigid divide between leaders and followers can create feelings of separation or mistrust, *miscommunication*- poor communication, whether unclear instructions or unmet expectations, can erode relationships, *cultural or personality differences*- diverse teams bring unique perspectives, but these differences can sometimes create misunderstandings, and *lack of effort-* building connection requires intentionality. When leaders or followers neglect this effort, relationships suffer.

John C. Maxwell's insight, "Connecting is the ability to identify with people and relate to them in a way that increases your influence with them," underscores the importance of fostering meaningful relationships. Whether you're a leader or a follower, connection is the foundation of trust, collaboration, and mutual growth.

By embracing connection, teams can transform challenges into opportunities, creating environments where everyone thrives. The Law of Connection emphasizes that effective followership and leadership hinge on strong, meaningful relationships. Here's how connection transforms teams and organizations: It *builds trust-* connection fosters an environment where trust flourishes. Teams are more likely to succeed when members feel secure in their relationships with leaders and peers. It *encourages open communication-* clear and honest communication minimizes misunderstandings and ensures alignment on goals and expectations. It *creates shared purpose-* when leaders and followers align on a shared mission, they develop a sense of unity that drives collaboration and motivation. And it *boosts morale and engagement-* empathy and understanding create a positive team culture where individuals feel valued and inspired.

HUMBLE INFLUENCE STORIES

The Bakery That Baked Connection into Its Success

When Ellie took over her family bakery, she quickly realized the business needed more than fresh bread and pastries to thrive—it needed a strong connection between her team and their customers. Despite the bakery's prime location, sales were declining, and her employees were disengaged.

Ellie decided to rebuild both her customer and employee relationships. She started by hosting a team meeting, emphasizing the bakery's deeper mission: creating a welcoming space where people could enjoy comforting food and meaningful connections. She shared her vision and invited her team to contribute ideas.

Built trust- Ellie took the time to listen to her employees, understanding their frustrations and aspirations. This effort opened a line of communication that had been missing.

Boosted morale and engagement- she discovered that several team members loved baking but felt disconnected from their customers. Together, they created a "Baker's Table" event, inviting customers to sample new recipes and give feedback.

Created shared purpose- Ellie began spending more time on the bakery floor, engaging directly with both staff and customers.

The transformation was profound. Employees became more engaged, taking pride in their work. Customers felt valued and started spreading the word about the bakery's personalized touch. Sales increased by 30 percent within six months, and the team's morale soared.

John C. Maxwell's quote, "People don't care how much you know until they know how much you care," encapsulates Emma's success. By prioritizing connection, she not only revived her business but also created a thriving community. Small businesses can build success by fostering connections both within their teams and with their customers.

A Tech Startup's Breakthrough – Building Trust in a Fast-Paced World

At a tech startup, Ryan, a junior software engineer, felt increasingly distanced from his manager, Claire. The team's rapid growth had created a divide between leadership and employees. Tasks were assigned with little explanation, and feedback was often overlooked in the rush to meet deadlines.

Frustrated but determined, Ryan decided to bridge the gap by building connections with Claire.

Encouraged open communication- Ryan requested a one-on-one meeting with Claire to better understand her vision and priorities. During the meeting, he shared constructive feedback, emphasizing his desire to help the team succeed.

Built trust- Ryan took the time to learn about Claire's challenges, such as managing investor expectations and scaling the company. This understanding helped him see the pressures she faced.

Boosted morale and encouragement- Ryan suggested creating a bi-weekly "feedback loop" session where the team could openly share ideas and updates with Claire. The initiative was well-received and implemented immediately.

The result was a more cohesive team. Claire began to rely on Ryan for insights, and the feedback loop fostered a culture of openness and innovation. Productivity increased, and the team delivered their project ahead of schedule. Connection is a two-way street. By proactively reaching out and demonstrating empathy, followers like Ryan can strengthen trust and improve team dynamics.

The Mentor Who Connected – A Leadership Journey with Purpose

Sophia, a nonprofit director, took on a mentorship role for Elena, a newly hired project coordinator. While Sophia was a seasoned leader, she understood that building a strong connection with Elena was key to her success.

Sophia invited Elena to shadow her for a week, allowing her to observe leadership decisions firsthand. During their time together Sophia:

Built trust- she asked about Elena's aspirations and challenges, taking a genuine interest in her career goals. This fostered trust and made Elena feel valued.

Created shared purpose- Sophia explained the organization's mission in detail, helping Elena see how her role contributed to their impact.

Boosted morale and encouragement- she scheduled weekly check-ins with Elena to provide guidance, feedback, and encouragement.

Elena blossomed under Sophia's mentorship. Within months, she led a successful fundraising campaign, exceeding targets by 20%. When asked about her rapid growth, Elena said, "Sophia didn't just guide me—she connected with me. She believed in me, and that belief inspired me to do my best." Effective leaders create lasting connections by investing time and energy in their followers.

KEY TAKEAWAY

The law of connection reminds us that relationships are the foundation of effective followership. By building strong, meaningful connections, followers can foster trust, enhance collaboration, and contribute to the success of their leaders, teams, and organizations.

In the next chapter, we'll explore the delicate balance of proximity in followership—how close is too close, and how distance can affect the leader-follower dynamic.

"Do not let any unwholesome talk come out of your mouths, but only what is helpful for building others up according to their needs, that it may benefit those who hear it" —Ephesians 4:29

(This verse encapsulates the importance of meaningful and uplifting communication.)

REFLECTION

Think about your current relationships with your leader and peers:
- Do you communicate openly and proactively?
- Have you invested time in understanding their perspectives?
- Are there barriers to connection that you can address?

"Proximity doesn't automatically create trust. It's the intention behind your presence that builds it."

—Simon Sinek

CHAPTER 7: HOW CLOSE SHOULD YOU GET?

The leader-follower relationship exists on a spectrum of proximity, ranging from distant to overly close, with each extreme presenting its own set of challenges. When the relationship is too distant, a lack of connection can breed misunderstandings, mistrust, and disengagement. Leaders may perceive distant followers as uninvolved or uninvested, which can weaken the team's dynamic and hinder productivity.

On the other hand, an overly close relationship between a leader and a follower can blur boundaries, leading to perceptions of favoritism. This proximity may also compromise the follower's ability to provide honest feedback, as the lines between personal and professional interactions become unclear. These challenges can create an imbalance that undermines both leadership and followership.

The ideal relationship lies in the middle of this spectrum, where collaboration flourishes. In this balanced dynamic, trust, communication, and mutual respect thrive, fostering a productive and supportive environment. At the same time, clear boundaries are maintained, ensuring that both leader and follower can contribute effectively to the team's success.

This sweet spot allows for the best of both worlds: connection without compromising professionalism.

There are benefits of a balanced proximity. When followers strike the right balance in their relationships with leaders, they unlock the full potential of their role and contribute significantly to the team's success. One of the most valuable outcomes of this balance is enhanced trust. A close-but-professional relationship fosters mutual confidence, making it easier for leaders and followers to share insights and work through challenges together.

This trust also paves the way for better feedback. When followers feel secure in their relationship with a leader, they are more likely to provide open and honest communication. Constructive feedback can flow without fear of retribution, creating an environment where issues are addressed proactively and growth becomes a shared goal.

Balanced relationships often lead to increased opportunities. Leaders are more inclined to involve trusted followers in decision-making processes and assign them to high-impact projects, recognizing their reliability and ability to contribute meaningfully. This dynamic not only benefits the individual follower but also strengthens the team as a whole.

A well-maintained balance between leaders and followers sets a positive tone that fosters respect and collaboration across the entire team. Strong team dynamics emerge when followers model professionalism and mutual respect, encouraging a culture of cooperation and shared success. Achieving this balance enhances not just the leader-follower relationship but the broader team environment.

Moses's relationship with his father-in-law, Jethro, offers a powerful example of balanced proximity. When Moses became overwhelmed by the demands of leading the Israelites, Jethro observed his struggles and offered advice in Exodus 18: 17-22: "What you are doing is not good. You and these people who come to you will only wear yourselves out." Jethro suggested that Moses delegate his responsibilities, allowing others to share the load. Moses trusted Jethro and implemented his advice, which transformed his leadership approach and improved the well-being of the entire community. Jethro's wisdom was rooted in his connection with Moses, but he maintained enough distance to provide honest feedback. There is a power of trust and objectivity in the leader-follower dynamic.

To find the right balance seek to understand the leader's style- some leaders prefer a collaborative approach, while others maintain more formal boundaries. *Adapt your proximity* to align with their preferences, *communicate openly-* discuss expectations and boundaries with your leader to ensure clarity and alignment, remain *focused on the mission-* keep the relationship centered on the organization's goals. This focus prevents personal dynamics from overshadowing professional priorities, *provide constructive feedback-* build trust by offering insights that support the leader's growth and decision-making, and *respect professional boundaries-*avoid overly personal interactions that could compromise the relationship's integrity.

There are risks in being too close: *perceived favoritism-* overly close relationships can create resentment among peers who feel overlooked or undervalued, *compromised objectivity-* followers who become too close to their leaders may struggle to provide constructive criticism or make unbiased decisions, *blurred boundaries-* a lack of professionalism can lead to misunderstandings or conflicts, damaging both the relationship and team dynamics.

In some situations, maintaining a greater distance is beneficial. When there is *conflict-* distance can provide space to resolve disagreements without escalating tension. If there is stress in the *team dynamics-* avoiding overly close relationships can ensure that no one feels excluded or undervalued. And if the *leader's style* is more formal in their relationships with followers, respect their preferences to maintain alignment.

Proximity in the leader-follower dynamic is a powerful tool, but only when managed with intentionality and care. Finding the right balance can foster trust, improve collaboration, and strengthen team morale.

Brené Brown reminds us, "Trust is earned in the smallest of moments." Your presence must be intentional and aligned with the mission.

The Law of Proximity teaches us that connection and boundaries are not mutually exclusive—they are complementary. By cultivating meaningful relationships while respecting professionalism, leaders and followers alike can create an environment of trust, collaboration, and success.

HUMBLE INFLUENCE STORIES

The Small Business Turnaround – Balancing Proximity for Success

Jenna owned a small café in a bustling downtown area. Her café had a loyal customer base, but internally, her team dynamics were strained. As a hands-on leader, Jenna was deeply involved in the day-to-day operations, working alongside her baristas, bakers, and servers. She prided herself on being approachable, but her closeness to the team had unintended consequences.

One of her baristas, Tim, began to feel that Jenna's frequent interactions with certain team members created favoritism. Other employees echoed this sentiment, noting that those who chatted with Jenna during shifts seemed to get better schedules and more input on decisions. The tension grew, and team morale suffered.

Recognizing the problem, Jenna sought advice from her mentor, who shared Brené Brown's wisdom: "Clear is kind. Unclear is unkind." Jenna realized she needed to establish clear boundaries while maintaining a sense of connection.

Some actions Jenna implemented:

Communicated openly- Jenna implemented regular team meetings where every member could voice their ideas and concerns. This leveled the playing field, ensuring all employees felt heard.

Focused on the mission- Jenna reminded her team of their shared goal: providing exceptional customer service. She emphasized how everyone's contributions were vital to the café's success.

Adapted her proximity- while Jenna remained friendly, she reduced informal, one-on-one conversations during shifts. Instead, she set aside time outside of work hours for team-building activities where everyone could participate equally.

Over time, the changes transformed the café's culture. Employees felt valued and appreciated, and customers noticed the improved morale. Jenna learned that proximity was a powerful tool, but only when balanced with fairness and transparency. In small businesses, leaders and followers must navigate proximity carefully. Building trust and collaboration requires maintaining boundaries that foster inclusivity and professionalism.

The Executive Assistant Who Found the Perfect Balance

Rachel was the executive assistant to David, the CEO of a growing healthcare startup. Their working relationship was unique—Rachel handled everything from managing David's calendar to coordinating high-stakes meetings. Over time, their close collaboration built trust, and David began seeking Rachel's input on strategic decisions.

However, Rachel noticed a growing issue: her colleagues viewed her as a gatekeeper who had too much influence over David. Some even began distancing themselves from her, assuming she was relaying their comments directly to the CEO. Rachel also started feeling uncomfortable about the blurred lines in her role—was she a decision-maker or simply an assistant?

To address the situation, Rachel reflected on her relationship with David. She applied key principles to recalibrate their dynamic:

Communicated openly- Rachel had a candid conversation with David about her role. She emphasized her commitment to supporting him while maintaining professional boundaries with the rest of the team.

Focused on the mission- during meetings, Rachel made an effort to redirect certain decisions to the appropriate department heads, reinforcing their authority and expertise.

Respected professional boundaries- Rachel scaled back on informal discussions with David, ensuring their interactions focused on his professional needs rather than personal opinions.

Rachel's recalibration paid off. Her colleagues began to see her as a neutral party, and her relationship with David became more effective. Rachel learned that while proximity could strengthen trust, maintaining boundaries ensured she remained a credible and respected team member. Followers who work closely with leaders must manage proximity intentionally to balance trust, professionalism, and team dynamics.

High Performing Sales Executive that Boosted Team Morale

Marcus was a high-performing sales executive at a tech startup. His rapport with the CEO, Sarah, was undeniable. They shared a vision for the company, often spent late hours brainstorming, and even bonded over their shared love of hiking.

But over time, Marcus's close relationship with Sarah began to raise eyebrows among his peers. They felt Marcus was receiving preferential treatment, which led to resentment and undermined team morale. On the other hand, Marcus found it challenging to maintain objectivity in his feedback to Sarah, fearing it might strain their relationship. Marcus took these action step:

Adapted his proximity- Marcus began to keep their brainstorming meetings within office hours.

Focused on the mission- he suggested to Sarah that they invite at least two other colleagues to participate in the brainstorming sessions knowing other colleagues had great ideas and they could increase creativity as well as keep meetings focused on the mission.

Provided constructive feedback- with more people in the brainstorming meeting it was helpful to keep notes and document suggestions in a shared document which allowed Marcus to offer his feedback without fear of straining the working relationship with Sarah.

This scenario is all too common in workplaces. Followers often struggle to find the right balance of proximity with their leaders—close enough to build trust and understanding, but distant enough to maintain professionalism and objectivity.

KEY TAKEAWAY

The leader-follower relationship thrives on balance. By cultivating trust and collaboration while maintaining professionalism, followers can build meaningful connections that drive individual and organizational success.

In the next chapter, we'll explore the principle of focusing on others, showing how prioritizing the needs of your leader and team can elevate your role and impact.

"I no longer call you servants, because a servant does not know his master's business. Instead, I have called you friends, for everything that I learned from my Father I have made known to you" —John 15:15

(This verse illustrates the balance of closeness and trust in relationships.)

REFLECTION

Ask yourself:
- Do I feel comfortable providing honest feedback to my leader?
- Are my peers comfortable with my relationship with my leader?
- Is my relationship with my leader contributing to or detracting from team success?

"You can have everything in life you want if you will just help enough other people get what they want."

—Zig Ziglar

CHAPTER 8: FOCUS ON THEM, NOT YOU

In every high-performing team, there's a common thread: the individuals involved prioritize the team's success over their own. This mindset is often the hardest part of followership to master. Our natural instinct is to focus on personal goals and recognition. Yet the most effective followers are those who turn their attention outward—to their leader, their peers, and the collective mission.

This chapter explores how focusing on others can transform your impact as a follower, elevate your team, and create a culture of collaboration and success.

Focusing solely on yourself can have serious consequences, undermining trust, team dynamics, and even your own personal growth. One common pitfall is seeking recognition above all else. Followers who prioritize personal accolades risk alienating their peers and fostering an environment of unnecessary competition, which can weaken the team's cohesion.

Another challenge arises when self-centered behavior undermines the team as a whole. By prioritizing individual goals over group objectives, followers may miss opportunities for collaboration, limiting the potential for collective success. This approach not only affects outcomes but also dampens the morale of the team, which thrives on shared effort and achievements.

Perhaps most damaging is the erosion of trust that occurs when a follower consistently places their own interests first. Leaders and peers are less likely to rely on individuals who fail to demonstrate loyalty to the team's mission. Trust is the foundation of any successful relationship, and when it is compromised, it becomes difficult to foster meaningful connections or achieve long-term growth.

Embracing a team-first mentality is essential for building trust, enhancing dynamics, and realizing true success.

The story of Jonathan and David in the Bible offers a powerful example of selflessness.

Jonathan, the son of King Saul, was next in line for the throne. Yet he recognized that David was chosen by God to lead Israel. Instead of clinging to his own ambitions, Jonathan supported David, even risking his life to protect him. Jonathan's focus wasn't on his personal gain but on the greater good. His loyalty and humility strengthened David's journey and left a lasting legacy of friendship and faithfulness.

Years after Jonathan's passing, David's commitment to their friendship remained steadfast. In 2 Samuel 9, David actively sought to show kindness to anyone left in Jonathan's household. He discovered Mephibosheth, Jonathan's son, who was crippled in both feet and living in obscurity.

Instead of seeing him as a threat to the throne, David restored Mephibosheth's inheritance and invited him to dine at the king's table for the rest of his life. This act of grace mirrors the faithfulness of God and exemplifies how true influence extends beyond personal ambition.

Jonathan's selflessness laid the foundation for David's kingship, and David's kindness ensured that Jonathan's legacy lived on. Their story is a testament to the power of loyalty, humility, and God-honoring influence.

Serving the mission begins with understanding your team's goals and aligning your efforts to support them. Success is about more than just completing individual tasks—it's about contributing to the bigger picture. For example, a marketing assistant who focuses on the success of an entire campaign rather than just ticking off their own responsibilities is more likely to make meaningful contributions that drive the team forward.

Supporting your leader is another critical aspect of effective followership. Anticipating their needs and looking for ways to make their role easier demonstrates commitment to the team's success. A project manager who identifies potential risks early and offers practical solutions not only earns the trust of their leader but also ensures the team remains on track.

Empowering your peers is equally important. Offering help, sharing knowledge, and celebrating the achievements of others strengthens team dynamics. For instance, a developer who takes time to mentor a junior teammate not only enhances team performance but also fosters stronger relationships and a sense of collaboration.

Finally, practicing empathy is essential for building trust and fostering a positive team environment. Taking the time to understand the challenges others face and approaching interactions with compassion can make a profound difference. Simply listening to a colleague's concerns or offering support during a difficult moment builds trust and promotes a culture of collaboration and mutual respect.

Together, these practices create a foundation for a thriving and successful team.

Shifting your focus outward has profound benefits: it *builds trust*-leaders and peers trust followers who prioritize the team's success over personal gain and *collaboration strengthens*- a focus on others fosters mutual support, creating a team culture where everyone thrives. Outward focus *elevates performance*- when you prioritize the mission and the people around you, your contributions have a greater impact and it *develops leadership qualities*- by serving others, you cultivate empathy, communication, and problem-solving skills—key traits of effective leaders.

Focusing on others doesn't mean neglecting yourself. To be an effective follower, you must also take care of your own well-being. It is important to *set boundaries*, to be clear about your limits to avoid burnout. To *prioritize self-care*, you have to take time to recharge physically, emotionally, and mentally, and be able to *communicate your needs*- effective relationships are built on mutual understanding. Don't hesitate to ask for support when needed.

A team is "we" not "I". The language of "I" isolates and diminishes a team. It is important to shift the focus from "I" to "we". This shift can happen when you focus on *serving the mission-* understand the overarching goals and align your efforts to support them, *support your leader-* anticipate your leader's needs and take proactive steps to make their role easier., *empower peers-* share knowledge, offer help, and celebrate the successes of others, and *practice empathy-* understand the challenges your leader and peers face, and approach interactions with compassion.

HUMBLE INFLUENCE STORIES

The Collaborative Marketing Manager – A Mid-Sized Business Transformation

At Horizon Tech, a mid-sized software company, tension was brewing within the marketing department. The team had just launched a new product, but the lack of collaboration and an "every person for themselves" mindset was apparent. Each member focused on their individual contributions, often neglecting the bigger picture.

Among them was Karen, the marketing manager, known for her humility and team-first mentality. As the team struggled to align, Karen decided to lead by example, embodying John C. Maxwell's quote: "Teamwork makes the dream work, but a vision becomes a nightmare when the leader has a big dream and a bad team." Karen did the following:

> *Served the mission-* Karen called a team meeting and shared a simple yet powerful message: "Our success is measured by how well we achieve the company's goals, not by individual accolades." She reframed the product's marketing campaign as a collective effort, highlighting the need for unity.

Empowered peers- Karen encouraged her team to share ideas without fear of judgment. When a junior marketer, Sam, proposed a social media strategy, Karen praised his creativity and asked him to lead the initiative. This move boosted Sam's confidence and inspired others to contribute.

Supported her leader- Karen anticipated the Chief Marketing Officer's needs by preparing detailed campaign updates and identifying potential risks before they escalated. Her proactive approach earned the CMO's trust and set an example for her peers.

Elevated performance- At every milestone, Karen acknowledged her team's contributions, ensuring everyone felt valued. She initiated a "Team Spotlight" email series, where individual achievements were recognized company wide.

By prioritizing the team's success over her own, Karen transformed the department's dynamics. The product campaign surpassed expectations, increasing engagement by 40 percent. The team, once fragmented, became cohesive and motivated. Karen's actions demonstrated that focusing on others fosters trust, collaboration, and shared success. In mid-sized businesses, a leader's outward focus can turn dysfunction into harmony, aligning teams with the mission and elevating their performance.

The Selfless Nurse – Putting the Mission First

In the fast-paced environment of St. Mary's Hospital, Daniel, a seasoned nurse, was a quiet yet powerful example of selfless followership. While other staff members often sought recognition for their contributions, Daniel's focus was always on his patients, colleagues, and the hospital's mission. Daniel did the following:

Practiced empathy- Daniel went beyond his job description to ensure patients felt cared for. During a particularly chaotic shift, he noticed a patient's family struggling to understand the treatment plan. Instead of delegating, Daniel patiently explained the procedure, easing their concerns and building trust.

Empowered peers- when a new nurse, Emily, joined the team, she felt overwhelmed by the ward's intensity. Daniel volunteered to mentor her, teaching her time-management techniques and how to handle high-pressure situations. Emily later credited Daniel with her ability to thrive in the role.

Supported his leaders- Daniel consistently anticipated the doctors' requirements during critical procedures, preparing equipment and organizing patient records before being asked. His readiness saved time and reduced errors, earning him respect across the hospital.

Served the mission- despite his contributions, Daniel never sought credit. When a colleague praised his efforts during a staff meeting, he redirected the recognition to the entire team, emphasizing their collective achievement.

Daniel's selflessness inspired others to adopt a similar mindset. The ward became more cohesive, with staff members supporting each other rather than competing. Patient satisfaction scores increased, and the hospital recognized the ward as a model of teamwork and excellence. Daniel's story illustrates that focusing on others, whether patients or peers, can elevate an entire team. By serving the mission and those around him, Daniel became a catalyst for positive change.

You can *build trust through selflessness-* focusing on the needs of others fosters trust. Leaders and peers are more likely to rely on those who prioritize the team's goals over personal recognition and *strengthen collaboration-* when followers empower their peers and leaders, they create a culture of mutual support. Collaboration becomes the norm, leading to greater success.

You will also be *developing leadership skills-* serving others hones critical skills such as empathy, communication, and problem-solving, preparing followers for future leadership roles which will *amplify your impact-* selfless actions often have a ripple effect, inspiring others and driving the collective success of the team or organization.

Practices to keep your focus outward:

Daily acts of service- identify one small way to support a colleague or leader each day. Reflect on how your actions contribute to the team's success.

Gratitude practice- write down three strengths you admire in your colleagues each week. Share this appreciation with them to strengthen your relationships.

Team success journaling- keep track of team achievements and the contributions of your peers. Use this to remind yourself of the collective effort behind success.

John C. Maxwell's quote, "Leadership is not about titles, positions, or flowcharts. It is about one life influencing another," encapsulates the essence of selfless followership. By focusing on the mission and the people around you, you not only elevate your team but also grow as a leader in your own right. The impact of your actions will ripple beyond individual contributions, inspiring others and driving collective success.

KEY TAKEAWAY

Effective followership is about prioritizing others—their needs, the team's goals, and the organization's mission. By focusing outward, you build trust, strengthen relationships, and elevate your impact.

In the next chapter, we'll explore how to gain substantial empowerment as a follower by taking initiative, embracing accountability, and demonstrating value.

"...whoever wants to become great among you must be your servant, and whoever wants to be first must be your slave— just as the Son of Man did not come to be served, but to serve, and to give his life as a ransom for many" —Matthew 20:26-28

(Focusing on others reflects Christ's model of servant leadership.)

REFLECTION

Ask yourself:
- Am I actively contributing to my team's success, or am I focused on my own recognition?
- How can I better support my leader and peers?
- What steps can I take to align my actions with the mission?

"Do what you can, with what you have, where you are."

—Theodore Roosevelt

CHAPTER 9: HOW TO GAIN SUBSTANTIAL EMPOWERMENT

Empowerment often feels like something granted by those in authority—a privilege bestowed on a select few. But in reality, empowerment is something followers can actively cultivate. It's not about waiting for permission but about demonstrating initiative, accountability, and value.

This chapter explores the strategies for gaining substantial empowerment as a follower, showing how you can position yourself as an indispensable contributor while driving progress within your organization.

Empowerment is the process of gaining the confidence, trust, and authority to take meaningful action. For followers, empowerment means:being trusted by your leader to make decisions, taking ownership of your role and responsibilities, and influencing outcomes and creating opportunities for success. Empowerment isn't something that simply happens—it's actively earned and cultivated.

To gain empowerment, followers must first adopt the right mindset of proactivity, accountability, and growth orientation. With proactivity, empowered followers don't wait for direction; they anticipate needs, identify opportunities, and take action. Accountability takes ownership of your work and its outcomes; it is essential for earning trust and respect. And growth orientation allows for viewing challenges as opportunities for learning and improvement and fosters confidence and capability.

Queen Esther's story in the Bible is a powerful example of empowerment. When the Jewish people faced annihilation, Esther took a bold step. She approached the king uninvited—a risky move that could have cost her life.

Esther's courage didn't come from a formal position of power; it came from her commitment to her people and her willingness to take initiative. Her proactive approach saved an entire nation.

This story reminds us that empowerment begins with action, not authority.

Empowerment is not a one-time achievement—it's an ongoing cycle of growth and contribution. To earn empowerment, focus on these pillars: initiative, value, and trust. *Take initiative-* empowered followers identify problems and offer solutions. Taking initiative shows your commitment to the team's success. *Demonstrate Value-* leaders empower followers they trust to deliver results. To build that trust; develop expertise in your role, consistently meet or exceed expectations, and seek feedback and use it to improve. *Build trust-* Trust is built on strong relationships. Focus on communicating openly and honestly with your leader, showing reliability and integrity in your actions, and collaborating effectively with peers.

EMPOWERMENT-IMPACT CYCLE

As this cycle continues, your influence and contributions will grow exponentially.

Take initiative
Identify opportunities and act on them.

Gain More Responsibility
Use your success to secure greater opportunities for impact.

Demonstrate Value
Show the results of your efforts. .

Build Trust
Earn your leader's confidence through consistent performance.

Some followers find it challenging to gain empowerment due to a mix of external and internal barriers. One common obstacle is micromanagement. When a leader struggles to delegate responsibilities, it can stifle a follower's ability to take initiative. In such cases, building trust is essential. Followers can demonstrate reliability by consistently delivering high-quality work and keeping their leaders informed of their progress, showing they are capable of handling tasks independently.

Another barrier is a lack of confidence. Followers who doubt their abilities may hesitate to step into more empowered roles. The key to overcoming this is focusing on small wins. By taking on manageable tasks and celebrating successes along the way, followers can gradually build their confidence while learning valuable lessons from any missteps.

Organizational culture can also hinder empowerment. In environments where empowerment is not a priority, followers may feel their contributions go unnoticed or unappreciated. Seeking out allies and mentors within the organization can make a significant difference.

These advocates can provide guidance, highlight opportunities, and help amplify a follower's contributions, even within challenging workplace dynamics.

By addressing these barriers with intentionality and persistence, followers can navigate the challenges to empowerment and create pathways for growth and meaningful impact.

While followers play an active role in seeking empowerment, leaders carry the important responsibility of creating an environment where empowerment can truly thrive. One way leaders foster this is by delegating responsibility, allowing followers to take ownership of meaningful tasks that contribute to the organization's success. By entrusting followers with significant responsibilities, leaders not only empower them but also demonstrate confidence in their abilities.

Providing resources is another critical aspect of effective leadership. Ensuring followers have the tools, training, and support they need to succeed sets them up for meaningful contributions and reinforces their sense of value within the team. Alongside this, encouraging decision-making is essential. Leaders who trust their followers to make choices within their scope of responsibility show respect for their judgment and create a culture of autonomy.

Finally, recognizing achievements is vital in reinforcing empowerment. Acknowledging and celebrating the contributions of followers not only boosts morale but also motivates the team to continue striving for excellence. Together, these actions by leaders cultivate a supportive and empowering environment where followers can thrive and reach their full potential.

HUMBLE INFLUENCE STORIES

Empowerment in Action – A Large Corporation's Product Innovation

At Summit Tech, a multinational corporation specializing in cloud-based solutions, the product development team was known for its rigid hierarchy. Junior team members often felt their voices were unheard, relegated to executing tasks without meaningful involvement in decision-making.

Amid this environment, Alex, a junior software engineer, saw an opportunity to challenge the status quo. While working on a complex project for a new AI-driven analytics tool, Alex noticed inefficiencies in the current development framework. Instead of merely flagging the issues, he decided to take action:

Took initiative- Alex studied alternative frameworks that could streamline the process, identifying one that had proven effective in similar use cases.

Built trust- he created a detailed presentation, outlining the benefits of adopting the new framework, potential challenges, and a phased implementation plan.

Demonstrated value- Alex pitched his idea during a team meeting, confidently addressing questions and concerns from senior engineers and the project manager.

Alex's initiative impressed the project manager, who not only approved the framework change but also tasked Alex with leading its integration. The new process reduced development time by 25 percent and improved overall team efficiency. Alex's actions positioned him as a trusted contributor, earning him greater responsibilities and an invitation to join the company's innovation council.

Napoleon Hill's quote, "Don't wait. The time will never be just right," encapsulates Alex's success. By taking initiative and acting decisively, he gained empowerment and made a lasting impact on the organization. In large corporations, empowerment often starts with taking calculated risks and demonstrating the value of your ideas.

From Good to Great – Empowerment in a Mid-Sized Manufacturing Firm

At Titan Fabrics, a mid-sized textile manufacturer, operations supervisor Priya was a rising star known for her problem-solving abilities. Despite her competence, she often found herself stuck in the shadow of her senior managers, waiting for approval on decisions she could easily handle.

Determined to break this cycle, Priya applied the Empowerment-Impact Cycle's pillars:

Took initiative- when an unexpected supply shortage threatened a major order, Priya stepped up. She negotiated directly with suppliers and coordinated with the production team to adjust schedules, ensuring the order was completed on time.

Demonstrated value- Priya began tracking operational inefficiencies, identifying bottlenecks in the supply chain. She researched industry best practices and proposed solutions tailored to Titan's unique needs.

Built trust- she worked closely with her peers in production and logistics, fostering trust and collaboration. By involving them in her initiatives, she ensured buy-in and support.

Priya's actions didn't go unnoticed. Her ability to manage crises and drive improvements earned her a promotion to operations manager, with expanded authority over key processes. Empowerment in mid-sized businesses requires a proactive mindset, a commitment to building relationships, and the confidence to make decisions that align with organizational goals.

The Empowerment-Impact Cycle in a Nonprofit Organization

At Bright Futures, a nonprofit dedicated to youth education, Leliana was a program coordinator who felt limited by her role's constraints. Passionate about making a bigger impact, Leliana decided to create her own opportunities by demonstrating her value.
Leliana's Empowerment Journey:

Took initiative- Leliana noticed a gap in the organization's outreach strategy—schools in underserved areas weren't being reached effectively. She gathered data to confirm her observation and proposed a targeted outreach program.

Built trust- Leliana designed a pilot program, complete with a budget, timeline, and measurable outcomes. She pitched the idea to the executive director, emphasizing how the program aligned with the nonprofit's mission.

Demonstrated value- she secured approval and led the pilot program, which resulted in a 30 percent increase in school partnerships within three months.

Leliana's initiative earned her a new role as the organization's outreach director. Her success not only empowered her but also demonstrated the impact of proactive followership on organizational growth. Napoleon Hill's insight, "Strength and growth come only through continuous effort and struggle," reflects Leliana's journey. Her persistence and dedication transformed her role and the organization's impact. Empowerment in nonprofits often comes from aligning personal initiative with the organization's mission and delivering measurable results.

Empowerment is not about waiting for opportunities—it's about creating them. "Action is the real measure of intelligence," as qouted by Napoleon Hill. It underscores the importance of proactive followership. By embracing the principles of empowerment, you can position yourself as a trusted, capable, and impactful member of your organization. Empowerment is a journey, not a destination. With each step, you build confidence, expand your influence, and unlock new opportunities for growth and success.

Exercises for gaining empowerment:

Daily Ownership- identify one task each day where you can take full ownership. Commit to delivering results without relying on external direction.

Initiative Challenge- find one problem in your team or organization and propose a solution to your leader.

Feedback Journal- keep a journal of feedback you receive and track how you've applied it to improve your performance.

KEY TAKEAWAY

Empowerment isn't something followers wait for—it's something they earn through competence, initiative, and trust. By embracing the principles of empowerment, you can drive meaningful impact and position yourself as an indispensable contributor.

In the next chapter, we'll explore the concept of judgment—when to use it, how to refine it, and why it's essential for effective followership.

"But those who hope in the Lord will renew their strength. They will soar on wings like eagles; they will run and not grow weary, they will walk and not be faint" —Isaiah 40:31

(True empowerment comes from reliance on God's strength.)

REFLECTION

Ask yourself:
- Do I take initiative in my role, or do I wait for direction?
- How have I demonstrated value to my leader and team?
- What steps can I take to gain greater trust and responsibility?

"It is not fair to ask of others what you are not willing to do yourself."

—Eleanor Roosevelt

CHAPTER 10: TO JUDGE OR NOT TO JUDGE

In any role, judgment is essential. Whether it's choosing the best course of action, providing feedback to a leader, or navigating team dynamics, good judgment is a hallmark of effective followership. Yet, exercising judgment as a follower can feel risky. How do you know when to speak up and when to stay silent?

This chapter delves into the role of judgment in followership, exploring when and how to use it, how to refine it as a skill, and why it's critical to the success of both leaders and teams.

Judgment is a double-edged sword. Used wisely, it can foster better decisions, strengthen relationships, and improve outcomes. Used poorly—or withheld altogether—it can cause conflicts, erode trust, or lead to missed opportunities. For followers, good judgment means knowing when to support your leader unconditionally (discernment), when to raise concerns or provide alternative perspectives (timeliness), and how to do both without undermining the mission or team dynamics (diplomacy).

Effective followership hinges on the delicate balance between exercising sound judgment and maintaining respect for leadership. Followers must first understand their role, ensuring that their judgment serves to support rather than undermine the leader. The purpose of their insights and actions should always be to strengthen the team and advance its goals.

Thoughtful communication is also essential. Providing feedback is an important part of followership, but it must be delivered constructively and with respect. The way a follower communicates can build trust and foster collaboration, ensuring that their input is received as helpful rather than disruptive.

Trust in the leader's authority is a cornerstone of effective followership. Once a decision is made, even if it differs from a follower's perspective, it's important to align actions with the team's objectives. This commitment to the collective mission reinforces unity and ensures that individual opinions don't detract from shared success. Together, these practices create a dynamic where followers can exercise judgment while upholding the integrity of the leader-follower relationship.

When clarity is missing, followers must rely on their judgment to navigate uncertainty. Vague or conflicting instructions can stall progress, but by stepping back to clarify goals and determine the best course of action, followers can keep the team moving forward and aligned with its objectives.

When risks are present, thoughtful judgment becomes even more critical. Decisions that carry potential negative consequences require careful assessment, weighing the risks, and offering insights to mitigate challenges. This proactive approach not only safeguards the team but also reinforces a follower's value as a trusted contributor.

Good judgment is equally important when feedback is needed. Constructive input helps leaders refine their approach, adjust strategies, and ultimately make better decisions. Providing feedback in a thoughtful and respectful manner fosters an environment where continuous improvement becomes a shared responsibility.

During times of conflict, sound judgment plays a key role in resolving disputes. Handling disagreements in a way that aligns with the team's goals while preserving relationships ensures that challenges don't derail progress. In all these scenarios, the ability to use judgment effectively elevates the role of the follower, contributing to the team's success and cohesion.

In the Bible, Abigail, the wife of Nabal, demonstrated extraordinary judgment. When her husband foolishly insulted David, risking retaliation, Abigail quickly assessed the situation and acted with wisdom. She intercepted David with gifts and a heartfelt apology, convincing him to spare her household. David recognized her good judgment, saying, "Praise be to the Lord...who has sent you today to meet me. May you be blessed for your good judgment."

Abigail's story highlights the key aspects of judgment: *discernment* by recognizing the gravity of the situation, *timeliness* by acting swiftly to prevent disaster, and *diplomacy* by addressing the issue respectfully and constructively.

There are pitfalls with poor judgement. When you *act without full context* and jump to conclusions or make decisions without all the necessary information it can lead to errors.

If you *overstep boundaries* and challenge your leader without respect or tact you will damage that relationship and erode their trust. And becoming *paralyzed by over-analysis* by overthinking decisions that lead you to inaction, which is often worse than making a wrong choice, can also erode your leader's trust.

There are ways you can continually refine your judgment by *seeking diverse perspectives*- consult colleagues or mentors to gain a broader understanding of the situation. *Reflect on past decisions*- analyze your previous decisions. What worked well? What could you have done differently? *Ask questions* in moments of uncertainty. Ask clarifying questions to gather more information. Always *consider the impact*- before acting, think about how your decision or feedback will affect the team, leader, and organization.

Exercises to Develop Judgement:

Scenario practice- create hypothetical situations where judgment is required. Practice making decisions and discuss your reasoning with a mentor or peer.

Decision journaling- keep a record of significant decisions you make, including the context, reasoning, and results. Use this journal to identify patterns and areas for improvement.

Feedback role-play- Practice providing feedback in a role-playing scenario. Focus on delivering your message respectfully and constructively.

John C. Maxwell's insight, "The difference between average people and achieving people is their perception and response to failure," reminds us that judgment is not just about making the right decisions but learning and growing from every experience. By refining your ability to assess situations, communicate effectively, and act thoughtfully, you can use judgment as a powerful tool to navigate challenges, support your team, and create meaningful impact.

HUMBLE INFLUENCE STORIES

Navigating a Crisis in a Large Corporation – Judgment in Action

At GlobalTech, a multinational corporation specializing in renewable energy solutions, the executive leadership team had invested heavily in a new wind turbine model. The product was slated to launch at an international expo in just a few weeks.

Shelly, a senior engineer on the project, noticed an issue during a routine test. The turbine's internal components had a design flaw that could lead to inefficiencies under certain weather conditions. The flaw wasn't immediately apparent and addressing it would delay the launch—an outcome the leadership team wanted to avoid. Instead of sounding the alarm publicly, Shelly demonstrated sound judgment in how she handled the situation:

Discerned the situation- Shelly ran additional tests to confirm her findings and ensure she fully understood the scope of the issue.

Acted with timeliness- she requested a private meeting with her division head, explaining the flaw with data to back her claims. She also proposed a workaround to mitigate the risk without derailing the launch.

Used diplomacy- while Shelly was confident in her recommendation, she acknowledged the leadership's broader considerations, such as market expectations and financial investments.

The division head appreciated Shelly's approach and escalated the matter to the executive team. After careful deliberation, the team decided to implement the workaround for the launch while dedicating resources to refining the design post-expo. Shelly's judgment prevented a potential PR disaster while maintaining the company's timeline for the expo. Her actions earned her recognition as a trusted advisor, leading to her promotion to project manager for the turbine refinement initiative.

John C. Maxwell's quote, "Leaders become great, not because of their power, but because of their ability to empower others," underscores the value of Shelly's contributions. By exercising judgment wisely, she empowered her leaders to make better-informed decisions. In large corporations, good judgment requires balancing individual expertise with respect for the broader mission.

The Restaurant Manager's Conflict Resolution – Judging When to Intervene

At The Artisan Table, a high-end restaurant, Anna, the assistant manager, noticed growing tension between two senior chefs, Mark and

Elena. Their arguments over menu changes were becoming more frequent, impacting team morale and service quality.

As the assistant manager, Anna's role was primarily operational, but she recognized that resolving the conflict was essential for the restaurant's success. She also understood the delicacy of intervening in a matter involving senior staff. Anna approached this by:

Discerning the situation- Anna took time to observe the interactions and gather input from other staff members to understand the root cause of the conflict. She discovered that Mark valued tradition while Elena wanted to innovate—a clash of philosophies rather than personal animosity.

Implemented timeliness- instead of confronting the issue during a busy service, Anna scheduled a meeting with Mark and Elena during a quieter period.

Used diplomacy- in the meeting, Anna acted as a neutral mediator. She acknowledged both chefs' perspectives and encouraged them to find common ground. For example, she proposed a special menu featuring both classic and modern dishes, allowing each chef to showcase their strengths. After the initial resolution, Anna continued to check in with both chefs to ensure the conflict didn't resurface.

The special menu became a hit with customers and elevated the restaurant's reputation for creativity and versatility. Mark and Elena began collaborating more effectively, and the kitchen team regained its harmony. Anna's actions earned her the trust of the staff and positioned her as a key leader in the restaurant. Judgment isn't just about making decisions—it's about knowing when and how to intervene. Anna's ability to address the conflict thoughtfully preserved team dynamics and improved the restaurant's operations.

KEY TAKEAWAY

Judgment is an essential skill for effective followership. By exercising thoughtful, informed judgment, followers can support their leaders, navigate challenges, and drive the team's success.

"Do not judge, or you too will be judged. For in the same way you judge others, you will be judged, and with the measure you use, it will be measured to you" —Matthew 7:1-2

(This reinforces the importance of humility and caution in judgment.)

REFLECTION

Reflect on your last failure.
Ask yourself:
- What did you learn from it?
- How have you grown because of it?
- Is there anything that needs to be reconciled with anyone involved in it?

"You can accomplish anything in life, provided that you do not mind who gets the credit."

—Harry S. Truman

CHAPTER 11: WHO CARES WHO GETS THE CREDIT?

In a high-stakes product pitch at a marketing agency, Lisa, the team leader, stood before the client presenting a campaign that her team had spent weeks crafting. Halfway through the presentation, she paused and said, "This concept wouldn't exist without Jamie's creativity. His work on the visuals brought the entire campaign to life."

The room buzzed with admiration. Lisa's humility and willingness to share credit didn't just elevate Jamie—it solidified her as a leader who values her team.

This chapter focuses on one of the most overlooked aspects of followership: humility. By letting go of the need for personal recognition, followers not only foster trust and collaboration but also position themselves as indispensable contributors to their teams and organizations.

Recognition is a natural human desire. Being acknowledged for your efforts can boost self-esteem and reinforce your value. Yet, the pursuit of credit can become problematic when it *distracts from the mission, creates competition, or erodes relationships.* When individuals focus on personal accolades, they may lose sight of the team's goals. If there is a need for recognition it can foster rivalry rather than collaboration. Any personal gain that is prioritized over the team's success damages trust and camaraderie.

Humility in followership isn't about diminishing your contributions—it's about recognizing that success is rarely a solo achievement. When followers prioritize the team's success over personal recognition they *strengthen relationships, enhance team performance, and build leadership skills.* A culture of humility fosters trust and mutual support, leading to better outcomes. Followers who prioritize others demonstrate the qualities of great leaders: empathy, collaboration, and a focus on collective success. Leaders and peers appreciate followers who share credit and work collaboratively.

John the Baptist offers a profound example of humility. As a preacher and prophet, he amassed a significant following. Yet when Jesus began His ministry, John said in John 3:30, "He must increase, but I must decrease." John's willingness to step aside and let Jesus take the spotlight exemplifies true humility. His focus wasn't on his own legacy but on fulfilling his purpose. This mindset is essential in followership. Great followers care more about the mission's success than their own recognition.

The principles of humility in followership are essential for building trust, fostering collaboration, and creating a culture of shared success. At the heart of humility lies the ability to prioritize the mission over personal accolades. A hallmark of humility is celebrating others. Publicly recognizing the contributions of teammates strengthens relationships and fosters cohesion. Humility transforms team dynamics and paves the way for lasting success. Simon Sinek's insight captures the essence of this practice: *"The goal is not to be perfect by the end. The goal is to be better today."* Humility is not about diminishing yourself; it is about lifting others.

Humility doesn't mean denying your contributions. There are times when taking credit is appropriate: *when it's earned, when it's strategic and when it is shared.* Receiving credit for the work you've genuinely done is appropriate but also acknowledge the contributions of others in that work. There are times when highlighting your efforts can demonstrate your value and open doors for better collaboration.

To accept credit as part of a team, emphasizing the collaborative effort behind the success, celebrates others and builds trust in the team.

There are risks of hoarding credit. Self-centered behavior can damage relationships, eroding trust and making it difficult for teams to collaborate effectively. People are less likely to collaborate if someone takes undue credit. Leaders and peers notice if someone is consistently placing themselves above the team. Over time, leaders may hesitate to assign responsibilities to individuals who consistently prioritize their own recognition over the team's success. The long-term consequences of hoarding credit can also tarnish reputations, as patterns of self-promotion are difficult to overcome and can isolate individuals from their peers.

Sharing credit is foundational. By focusing on the team's mission and sharing credit generously, followers create a ripple effect of trust and collaboration. This mindset not only strengthens the team but also sets the stage for personal growth as a leader. Giving credit where it's due ensures contributions are fairly acknowledged, especially when presenting outcomes to leaders or stakeholders.

Adopting a practical strategy of sharing credit will strengthen the fabric of your organization. When you *acknowledge contributors publically*, in meetings or reports, it highlights the efforts of your peers and leaders. By *using the inclusive language of "we" instead of "I"* when discussing achievements it reinforces the team's role in the success. Going beyond just general praise by *recognizing specific contributions* shows genuine appreciation and fosters trust. And *expressions of gratitude*- thanking individuals for their support, collaboration, and unique contributions to the team reinforces the "we". These strategies will strengthen the team's morale and position you as a trusted collaborator.

Practicing humility requires intentionality and consistent effort. Small, practical steps can make a significant impact. For instance, taking time each day to identify and thank a colleague for their contributions reinforces gratitude and strengthens connections. Team reflection is another powerful practice. During meetings, setting aside time to discuss achievements as a group allows everyone to celebrate collective wins. Gratitude journaling at the end of each week is equally effective—writing down how others' efforts positively impacted your work encourages self-awareness and reciprocity.

Humility is contagious. When you model selflessness and celebrate others, you inspire those around you to do the same. This ripple effect transforms team dynamics, creating a culture of trust, collaboration, and shared success.

HUMBLE INFLUENCE STORIES

The Corporate Turnaround – Humility in a Large Corporation

At Orion Enterprises, a Fortune 500 logistics company, the supply chain division faced a significant crisis. Delays and inefficiencies in their international shipping operations had disrupted client deliveries, threatening key contracts. The CEO formed a task force led by Charlie, a senior operations manager, to resolve the issue.

Charlie brought together a diverse team of logistics experts, IT developers, and customer service managers to tackle the problem. While she led the team with confidence, her approach prioritized collaboration and humility:

Celebrated specific efforts- when a junior IT developer, Ravi, designed a tracking algorithm that reduced delays by 15 percent, Charlie publicly credited him during a leadership meeting. She emphasized how Ravi's innovation was integral to the team's success.

Expressed gratitude- as the team implemented solutions, Charlie consistently expressed gratitude for their collective efforts.

Used inclusive language- during a company-wide town hall, the CEO praised Charlie's leadership, but Charlie redirected the recognition: "This was a team victory! We all played a critical role."

Humility doesn't go unnoticed. Charlie's peers respected her more, and her team was motivated to continue excelling. Later, she was promoted to VP of Operations, with many citing her ability to inspire and empower others. "Leadership is not about being in charge. It is about taking care of those in your charge", Simon Sinek. By valuing her team over personal accolades, she elevated both the group's performance and her own leadership reputation. Even in large corporations, prioritizing team success and sharing credit fosters trust, collaboration, and long-term leadership growth.

The Marketing Campaign That Changed a Startup's Culture

In a fast-growing tech startup, Ethan, a marketing specialist, worked on a high-stakes product launch. His innovative content strategy played a pivotal role in the campaign's success, doubling pre-order numbers within two weeks.

However, Ethan's immediate supervisor, Daniel, presented the results to the executive team as if they were solely his achievement, failing to acknowledge Ethan. Frustrated but determined, Ethan chose humility and collaboration over confrontation. Ethan's awareness of the benefits of sharing credit enabled him to:

Expressed gratitude- instead of dwelling on the oversight, Ethan expressed gratitude for the opportunity to be part of the team. His belief in the product's impact mattered more than individual recognition.

Celebrated specific efforts- during a team meeting, Ethan acknowledged the contributions of the graphic designer and data analyst, saying, "Your work brought this strategy to life. This success is ours as a team."

Used inclusive language- Ethan scheduled a one-on-one with Daniel, respectfully addressing the lack of credit. He framed his feedback around improving team culture, saying, "When we celebrate everyone's contributions, we build trust and inspire better results."

Ethan's actions had a ripple effect. Daniel began recognizing team members more openly, realizing the value of collective acknowledgment. Ethan's humility and leadership potential were noticed by the COO, who assigned him to lead the company's next campaign. In startups, where recognition often feels critical for career growth, selflessness and humility can stand out as defining qualities. By focusing on the team's success, Ethan not only earned trust but also positioned himself as a future leader.

Humility is the foundation of strong followership and leadership alike. By intentionally recognizing others, focusing on the greater mission, and creating space for shared success, followers build trust, inspire their teams, and strengthen the fabric of the organization. True influence comes not from seeking the spotlight but from helping others shine.

KEY TAKEAWAY

Humility isn't about denying your worth—it's about celebrating the contributions of others and prioritizing the team's success. By sharing credit, you build trust, strengthen relationships, and foster a culture of collaboration.

In the next chapter, we'll explore the importance of authenticity in followership and why being yourself is one of the greatest assets you can bring to your team.

"So neither the one who plants nor the one who waters is anything, but only God, who makes things grow" —1 Corinthians 3:7

(This reminds us that success belongs to God, not individual efforts.)

REFLECTION

Reflect on your recent achievements.
Ask yourself:
- Who contributed to your success?
- How can you celebrate their efforts?
- Are there moments when you may have unnecessarily sought credit for yourself?

"Be yourself; everyone
else is already taken."
—Oscar Wilde

CHAPTER 12: IT'S OK TO BE YOU

This chapter explores the power of authenticity in followership. Authenticity in followership begins with a deep understanding of yourself—your values, strengths, and passions—and how these align with your role and contributions. Knowing yourself provides a foundation for meaningful engagement with your team and leader. Being yourself isn't just acceptable—it's essential. Embracing your individuality allows you to contribute in ways that no one else can.

Authenticity means embracing your unique qualities, values, and strengths. It's about showing up as your true self, not as a version of what you think others expect. Here's why authenticity matters in followership: it *builds trust*- leaders and peers trust followers who are genuine. Authenticity fosters credibility and strengthens relationships. It *enhances collaboration*- when followers bring their authentic selves to the team, they contribute diverse perspectives and ideas. It *drives fulfillment*- suppressing your true self can lead to dissatisfaction and burnout. Authenticity allows you to engage fully and find meaning in your work. And it *encourages innovation*- authenticity creates a safe space for creativity and risk-taking, driving innovation and problem-solving.

Open communication is a natural extension of authenticity. Sharing ideas and perspectives honestly while respecting the contributions of others creates an environment of trust and transparency. Followers who communicate openly demonstrate confidence in their unique voice while strengthening relationships within the team. At the same time, authenticity also requires the courage to accept imperfections. Rather than hiding flaws, authentic followers embrace them as part of their humanity. These imperfections, when acknowledged, can foster connection and relatability, reminding others that perfection is not required to make a meaningful impact.

Authenticity starts with self-awareness. Who are you? Reflect on your values, strengths, and passions. Ask yourself: What drives me? What do I naturally excel at? What brings me fulfillment? Authenticity allows you to *align your actions with values*- living and working in alignment with your core beliefs ensuring your decisions and behaviors reflect your values.

Focusing on the unique qualities you bring to the team allows you to *leverage your strengths*. Whether it's analytical thinking, empathy, or creativity, your strengths are your superpower. Authenticity doesn't mean being blunt—it means being genuine. By aligning your unique contributions with the broader objectives of the team, you honor both yourself and the collective purpose. Every follower brings unique skills and experiences to the table, and using those strengths strategically elevates the team as a whole.

Open communication is a natural extension of authenticity. Sharing ideas and perspectives honestly while respecting the contributions of others creates an environment of trust and transparency. It demonstrates confidence in your unique voice while strengthening relationships within the team.

No one is perfect, and acknowledging your weaknesses makes you more relatable and trustworthy.

By aligning your unique contributions with the broader objectives of the team, you honor both yourself and the collective purpose. Seeking feedback from trusted peers and leaders is a way to maintain balance, using their input to refine your approach while staying grounded in who you are. The balance of authenticity and adaptability is the mark of a strong follower. By knowing yourself, leveraging your strengths, and communicating openly, you not only become a valuable part of the team but also inspire others to embrace their own authentic contributions.

Before David became king, he was offered King Saul's armor to face Goliath. But David declined, saying in 1 Samuel 17:39, "I cannot go in these, because I am not used to them." Instead, he faced the giant with his sling and five smooth stones—tools he was familiar with as a shepherd. David's authenticity was key to his victory. His authenticity was that he had a firm reliance on God's past faithfulness, confidence in his abilities, and refusal to be something he was not. He didn't try to fight like Saul or anyone else. He relied on his own strengths and experiences, and it made all the difference. Like David, followers thrive when they embrace their unique qualities rather than trying to fit someone else's mold.

While authenticity is crucial, it must be balanced with adaptability. The balance of authenticity and adaptability is the mark of a strong follower. You can achieve that balance by *being respectful*- authenticity doesn't mean disregarding others' perspectives or needs. Balance being true to yourself with consideration for your team. Flexibility is key in followership but adapt in ways that align with your values and integrity, *adapt without losing yourself.* Use your unique qualities to contribute to the team's mission, *focus on shared goals.* Authenticity does not serve individual pride—it serves the mission. It should enhance collaboration, not detract from it. It's important to find a balance between staying true to yourself and adapting to the needs of the team. Flexibility, when grounded in integrity, allows followers to navigate challenges without losing sight of their core values.

Trying to be someone you're not can have serious consequences. Inauthenticity *damages trust and reduces engagement.* People can sense when someone is not genuine, which undermines relationships. Constantly pretending to be something you are not is emotionally exhausting and leads to disengagement. Suppressing your unique qualities means *missing out on opportunities* where those strengths could shine and the emotional toll of inauthenticity often leads to stress and *burnout.*

Embracing authenticity can be strengthened through practical reflection. Taking time to assess your values is a valuable exercise in understanding what drives you. Identifying your top three personal values and reflecting on how they guide your decisions can clarify your purpose and align your actions with your principles. A strengths inventory is another helpful tool, allowing you to identify the unique skills you bring to the team and how they can address current challenges. A weekly check-in offers an opportunity for ongoing growth: reflect on moments where authenticity made a difference—or where it may have been compromised—this helps to build awareness and strengthen your ability to lead and contribute as your most genuine self.

HUMBLE INFLUENCE STORIES

Authenticity in a Church Leadership Team

At Grace Community Church, the leadership team was preparing for its annual community outreach program. The team included Pastor James, known for his powerful sermons, and Mary, a youth leader with a quieter but deeply empathetic approach.

While planning the event, Pastor James encouraged the team to share ideas for improving engagement. Large inflatables! A stage with a live band! A skills clinic. Mary had a very different idea. "These are all great ideas and could be so much fun! What if we also offered a series of one-on-one mentoring sessions to build deeper relationships with attendees?"

Her idea was met with enthusiasm. The team realized that large-scale events and personal connections could complement each other. Mary was asked to spearhead the mentoring initiative. Mary embraced her authenticity.

Communicated openly- Mary acknowledged how much fun the ideas being shared were and respectfully added a very different idea.

Leveraged her strengths- her idea leaned into her empathetic nature.

Aligned actions with her values- she organized a series of small-group and individual sessions tailored to participants' unique needs.

The outreach program was a success, drawing in more participants than previous years. Many attendees praised the mentoring sessions, which helped them feel genuinely connected to the church. Mary's authenticity inspired other team members to explore new ideas, fostering a culture where everyone's strengths were valued. By choosing to embrace her authentic self, she contributed to the team's success and strengthened the church's community impact. In faith-based organizations, authenticity allows leaders and followers to serve with integrity, creating deeper connections and meaningful change.

A Large Corporation's Innovation Through Authenticity

At Zenith Pharmaceuticals, the R&D department was tasked with developing a groundbreaking medication for chronic pain relief. The team included Malik, a senior researcher, known for his meticulous attention to detail, and Jessica, a younger researcher whose creative thinking often challenged traditional approaches.

Jessica often felt her bold ideas were overshadowed by her peers' technical expertise. However, during a brainstorming session, the team hit a roadblock: their formula wasn't producing consistent results. Jessica hesitated but decided to share her unconventional idea—using a plant-based compound rarely explored in mainstream pharmaceuticals. Jessica's Authentic Contribution:

Leveraged her strengths- Jessica's background in alternative medicine informed her suggestion. Instead of trying to fit into the mold of her more experienced colleagues, she leaned into her unique expertise.

Communicated openly- Jessica respectfully presented research supporting the compound's potential, demonstrating its alignment with the company's mission of innovation.

The team adopted Jessica's idea, and after months of testing and refinement, the plant-based formula proved successful. The medication became a flagship product, earning industry recognition and boosting the company's reputation for innovative solutions. Jessica's authenticity not only solved a critical problem but also inspired her peers to approach challenges with openness and creativity.

Her ability to balance confidence in her ideas with humility and collaboration exemplifies the power of authenticity in driving organizational success. In large corporations, embracing diverse perspectives and staying authentic can lead to groundbreaking innovation and strengthen team cohesion.

Jim Collins saying, "True leadership only exists if people follow when they have the freedom not to" underscores the role of authenticity in inspiring others. When you bring your genuine self to your work, you encourage your team to do the same, creating a culture where trust and collaboration thrive. Authenticity isn't a weakness— it's a strength that fuels creativity, fosters relationships, and drives success. By being yourself, you not only elevate your contributions but also inspire others to reach their full potential.

KEY TAKEAWAY

Authenticity isn't just OK—it's essential. By being yourself, you bring unique value to your team, build trust, and find greater fulfillment in your work.

With this chapter, we conclude our exploration of effective follower-ship. But your journey doesn't end here—it's just beginning.

"I praise you because I am fearfully and wonderfully made; your works are wonderful, I know that full well" —Psalm 139:14

(This highlights the beauty of authenticity and being created uniquely by God.)

REFLECTION

Ask yourself:
- Am I showing up as my true self, or am I trying to meet others' expectations?
- How do my unique qualities and divine gifts contribute to my team's success?
- What steps can I take to align my actions with my values?

"Whatever you do, work
heartily, as for the Lord
and not for men."
—Colossians 3:23

CHAPTER 13:
WORKING WITH
ALL YOUR HEART

It's easy to view certain jobs as more meaningful than others. A pastor's sermon or a doctor's surgery might feel more impactful than folding laundry or writing reports. But the truth is that God values faithfulness in every role. When we approach our work with integrity, diligence, and a desire to honor Him, we reflect His character to those around us.

Paul's instruction in Colossians 3:23 is both simple and profound, "Whatever you do, work at it with all your heart, as working for the Lord, not for human masters." He calls us to approach every task—whether mundane or monumental—as if we are doing it directly for the Lord. This shift in perspective elevates the significance of even the most routine activities. Whether we are answering emails, caring for children, or leading a team, our work becomes a sacred act when we do it for God's glory.

When we approach our tasks with diligence and view our efforts as offerings to the Lord, we embody the humility, commitment, and reliability that great followers demonstrate. Effective followership isn't about seeking recognition but about aligning with a mission and contributing meaningfully, no matter the role or task. By working with all our heart for God, we elevate the impact of our followership and inspire those around us to do the same.

Jesus Himself provides the ultimate example of working with all one's heart. Before beginning His public ministry, Jesus spent years as a carpenter. He shaped wood into functional and beautiful creations, performing His work with care and precision. Though the Gospels do not detail His time as a tradesman, we can imagine that He approached each task with the same excellence and love that characterized His ministry.

Jesus' example reminds us that no work is beneath us, and no task is too small to bring glory to God. The same hands that later healed the sick and broke bread with thousands first worked with simple tools, crafting tables and chairs for ordinary people. In His humility and faithfulness, Jesus dignified the ordinary and transformed it into an act of worship.

HUMBLE INFLUENCE STORIES

A Nurse's Night Shift

Grace worked the night shift at a bustling city hospital. As a nurse, her duties ranged from administering medications to comforting patients in pain. The hours were long, and the emotional toll was immense. Sometimes, her work felt thankless—most patients were too ill or overwhelmed to notice her kindness.

One night, Grace cared for an elderly woman, Mrs. Latham, who was recovering from surgery. Despite Grace's efforts, Mrs. Latham was irritable and demanding, complaining about everything from the food to the temperature of the room. Grace struggled to remain patient, but as she walked into the breakroom, feeling discouraged, she remembered the verse her mother had often quoted: "Whatever you do, work heartily, as for the Lord and not for men."

Grace prayed silently, asking God to help her see her work as service to Him. With a renewed heart, she returned to Mrs. Latham's room, gently adjusting her blankets and listening to her concerns. Over the next few hours, Grace's attitude of care softened Mrs. Latham's demeanor. Before Grace's shift ended, the woman grabbed her hand and whispered, "Thank you for treating me with such kindness." Though Grace hadn't sought praise, those words confirmed what she had realized: her work wasn't just about medical tasks; it was about reflecting God's love to those she served, even in the smallest ways.

A Teacher's Impact

Derrick was a middle-school math teacher in a small rural town. He loved teaching but often found himself discouraged by the challenges—underfunded classrooms, disengaged students, and the weight of knowing that some of his students faced difficult lives at home.

One afternoon, Derrick stayed late to grade papers. As he sifted through the stack of quizzes, his eyes fell on a note written on the bottom of one paper. It read: "Thank you for believing in me, Mr. B. You make math less scary." Tears welled up in his eyes. That evening, as Derrick reflected on his calling, he came across Colossians 3:23 in his devotional reading. It struck him deeply. He realized that his work was not just about equations and exams; it was an opportunity to show love, patience, and encouragement to his students.

The next day, Derrick entered the classroom with a renewed sense of purpose. He began incorporating more creative activities to engage his students and offered one-on-one help after class. Over time, his dedication transformed not only his classroom but also the students' attitudes. Many began to thrive, both academically and personally, inspired by his genuine care and unwavering effort. Through his work, Derrick found fulfillment, knowing that he was serving God by shaping young minds and hearts, one lesson at a time.

Humble Excellence in the Modern World

Consider the story of Mario, a janitor at a large office building. To many, Marcio's job seemed insignificant. But Mario approached his work with joy and a deep sense of purpose. Every night, as he mopped floors and emptied trash bins, he prayed for the people who would occupy the space the next day. He believed his work contributed to a clean and welcoming environment where others could thrive. One day, an executive noticed Mario's cheerful demeanor and asked him what kept him so positive. Mario simply replied, "I'm not just cleaning floors. I'm serving God through my work."

His words left a lasting impact, inspiring the executive to re-evaluate his own approach to leadership. Mario's faithfulness in his unseen work became a testimony of God's love and a source of inspiration to others.

As we embrace the truth of Colossians 3:23, may we find joy, purpose, and fulfillment in our work, knowing that everything we do can reflect God's glory and serve His greater plan.

KEY TAKEAWAY

Colossians 3:23 is painted over the threshold of my office – in a place where anyone entering our business can clearly see it. In my experience over the past few years, it's clear that verse connects with people. It's kind of an "aha" moment of realizing that there's something palpably different about my team and our company culture.

Here are four ways you live out working at with all your heart, as working for the Lord:

Dedicate Your Work to God- begin each day with prayer, offering your tasks to God and seeking His guidance.

Strive for Excellence- whether your work is celebrated or unseen, commit to doing it well, knowing that it honors God.

Look for Opportunities to Serve- view your work as a way to bless others, whether through your attitude, quality, or encouragement.

Cultivate Gratitude- focus on the blessings in your work, no matter how small, and thank God for the opportunity to contribute.

"Let the favor of the Lord our God be upon us, and establish the work of our hands upon us; yes, establish the work of our hands" —Psalm 90:17

(This reminds us that when we work with all our heart for the Lord, His favor rests upon us, giving purpose, significance, and lasting impact to even the simplest tasks we undertake.)

REFLECTION

Think about your daily tasks.
- Are there areas where you've felt disheartened or undervalued?
- How might your perspective change if you approached those tasks as if working directly for the Lord?

CHAPTER 14: CONCLUSION: THE GREATEST FOLLOWER: JESUS CHRIST'S PATH TO ULTIMATE LEADERSHIP

Throughout His life, Jesus Christ exemplified the principles of followership, demonstrating that the path to true leadership is paved with humility, obedience, and a servant's heart. By perfectly embodying the qualities of an ideal follower, Jesus became the ultimate leader, inspiring billions across history and shaping the course of humanity.

This summary draws on the core themes of the book to show how Jesus lived out the ultimate model of followership, revealing why He became the greatest leader the world has ever known.

Submission to a greater mission- one of the defining aspects of Jesus' life was His unwavering submission to the will of God the Father. He made it clear that His purpose was not to pursue personal ambition but to fulfill a divine mission.

"For I have come down from heaven not to do my will but to do the will of him who sent me" —John 6:38

This obedience is the essence of followership—aligning one-self with a purpose greater than personal desires. Even in the face of immense suffering, such as in the Garden of Gethsemane, Jesus prayed, "Not my will, but yours be done" (Luke 22:42). His submission demonstrated ultimate trust, humility, and commitment to God's plan.

True followers prioritize the mission above themselves, trusting in a greater purpose.

Servant leadership- Jesus led by serving. Whether washing His disciples' feet (John 13:12-17) or healing the sick and feeding the hungry, His actions revealed that leadership is about elevating others, not seeking status or power.

"Be like the Son of Man. He did not come to be served. Instead, he came to serve others. He came to give his life as the price for setting many people free" —Matthew 20:28

By embracing the role of a servant, Jesus flipped the world's concept of leadership on its head. He showed that a leader's authority stems from their willingness to serve others selflessly.

Followership rooted in service transforms leadership into an act of love and sacrifice.

Humility and authenticity- Jesus never sought personal glory. Instead, He consistently pointed people toward God. Despite His divine nature, He humbled Himself to live among humanity, experiencing life's struggles and serving the least and the lost.

"In your relationships with one another, have the same mindset as Christ Jesus: Who, being in very nature God, did not consider equality with God" —Philippians 2:5-7

Jesus' humility and authenticity resonated with those He encountered, making His leadership deeply personal and transformative. His authenticity inspired trust, as people could see He genuinely cared for them.

Great leaders are grounded in humility and gain influence through their authenticity and integrity.

Empathy- throughout His ministry, Jesus demonstrated unparalleled empathy. He wept with those who mourned, forgave those who sinned, and reached out to the marginalized. His ability to connect with people on a deeply personal level was a cornerstone of His leadership.

"Come to me, all you who are weary and burdened, and I will give you rest" —Matthew 11:28

By meeting people where they were and addressing their unique needs, Jesus showed that effective followership and leadership begin with understanding others.

Empathy bridges the gap between leaders and followers, creating trust and fostering connection.

Sacrifice for the greater good- The ultimate act of followership—and leadership—came when Jesus sacrificed Himself on the cross. His obedience to God and His love for humanity culminated in the ultimate display of selflessness.

"Greater love has no one than this: to lay down one's life for one's friends" —John 15:13

Through His sacrifice, Jesus not only fulfilled His mission but also paved the way for salvation, transforming the lives of countless followers across generations. His death and resurrection exemplify that true leadership often requires personal sacrifice for the benefit of others.

Sacrificial followership creates a legacy that inspires others to rise to their potential.

Empowering others- Jesus didn't just lead—He empowered His disciples to carry on His work. He invested in them, taught them, and gave them the authority to preach, heal, and spread the Gospel. Before His ascension, He gave them the Great Commission:

"Go and make disciples of all nations, baptizing them in the name of the Father and of the Son and of the Holy Spirit" — Matthew 28:19

By trusting His followers with the mission, Jesus demonstrated the ultimate act of leadership: equipping others to lead. His empowerment of the disciples turned a small group of individuals into a global movement.

Great leaders empower their followers, trusting them to continue the mission and multiply its impact.

Transforming others through followership- Jesus' ability to lead sprang directly from His perfect followership. His relationship with God the Father was one of complete trust, obedience, and alignment. By modeling what it meant to follow, He transformed His disciples into leaders who would go on to change the world.

"In your relationships with one another, have the same mindset as Christ Jesus: Who, being in very nature God, did not consider equality with God something to be used to his own advantage; rather, he made himself nothing by taking the very nature of a servant, being made in human likeness.And being found in appearance as a man, he humbled himself by becoming obedient to death—even death on a cross!" —Philippians 2:5-8

Jesus' greatness stemmed from His conscious choice to obey God's will, even when it meant enduring unimaginable hardship. His discipline as a follower laid the foundation for His unparalleled leadership. *The best leaders are those who have first mastered the art of followership.*

KEY TAKEAWAY

In a world that often glorifies self-promotion and power, Jesus' example reminds us that the greatest leaders are those who put others before themselves, serve with humility, and remain steadfast in their purpose. His life challenges us to rethink what it means to lead and to embrace the strength found in authentic, selfless followership.

By following His example, we can not only become better followers but also inspire others to greatness, fulfilling the higher calling of both followership and leadership.

"Every knee should bow, in heaven and on earth and under the earth, and every tongue acknowledges that Jesus Christ is Lord, to the glory of God the Father" —Philippians 2:9-11

(This affirms Christ's ultimate leadership through humility and servanthood.)

REFLECTION

The Model for Leadership Today

Jesus' life provides a timeless blueprint for leadership rooted in followership:

Prioritize the Mission- align your actions with a purpose greater than yourself.

Lead Through Service- put the needs of others first, modeling humility and love.

Be Authentic- embrace your unique gifts and values to build trust and inspire others.

Empower Others- equip those around you to grow and lead, multiplying your impact.

Jesus showed that followership isn't a sign of weakness—it's the foundation of transformative leadership. By living as the ultimate follower, He became the ultimate leader, leaving a legacy that continues to shape the world.

"The world is moved
not only by the mighty
shoves of the heroes but
also by the aggregate of
the tiny pushes of each
honest worker."

—Helen Keller

EPILOGUE: FOLLOWING FROM WITHIN

As the final page turns on this journey, one truth shines brightly: followership is not a secondary role—it's a cornerstone of success. The world often celebrates leaders, but it's the quiet strength of followers that drives missions forward, builds bridges, and shapes legacies.

Throughout this book, we've redefined followership, not as passive compliance but as active, intentional participation in the shared goals of a team, an organization, or a community. Great followers aren't born—they're developed through purpose, practice, and a commitment to growth.

The Principles of Followership

Start with the Mission- like Joshua following Moses or the janitor at NASA, purpose gives meaning to our work and aligns our efforts with something greater than ourselves.

Cultivate Relationships- connection is the foundation of trust. Building strong, collaborative relationships fosters communication, loyalty, and success.

Balance Proximity with Professionalism- effective followers are close enough to support their leaders but maintain the objectivity needed to offer constructive feedback and act independently.

Focus on Others- by prioritizing the needs of your leader, peers, and team, you create a culture of trust, collaboration, and shared achievement.

Seek Empowerment through Action- empowerment isn't granted—it's earned through competence, initiative, and accountability.

Exercise Sound Judgment- good judgment is a hallmark of followership. It enables you to contribute meaningfully while respecting the authority and vision of your leader.

Share the Spotlight- humility is a strength. Celebrating others builds trust, strengthens relationships, and elevates the entire team.

Be Authentic- your unique qualities are your greatest asset. By embracing authenticity, you build trust, contribute meaningfully, and inspire others to do the same.

Your Next Steps

Followership is a journey, not a destination. As you move forward, consider these steps to deepen your impact:

Embrace Your Role- take pride in being a follower. Recognize the value you bring to your team, leader, and mission.

Apply the Principles- reflect on the lessons from this book and implement them in your daily work. Start small—celebrate a teammate, take initiative on a project, or align your efforts with your organization's goals.

Lead from Within- followership and leadership are not opposites—they're intertwined. By leading from within, you inspire trust, drive success, and contribute to a legacy that goes beyond titles and accolades.

HUMBLE INFLUENCE: A Movement

In a quiet church sanctuary one Sunday morning, a pastor spoke on the importance of followership. He shared a story about Joshua, who spent decades faithfully serving Moses before leading the Israelites into the Promised Land. The pastor's voice echoed in the stillness, "Joshua's story isn't about waiting in the shadows—it's about preparation. His followership forged the character and skills he needed to lead."

For those in the congregation, the message hit home. The idea that following with humility and purpose could shape someone into a leader was a revelation. One young woman, Sarah, sat in quiet reflection. She had been wrestling with feelings of insignificance in her workplace, unsure if her contributions mattered. But that morning, she realized her role as a follower was a sacred opportunity to grow and serve.

The lessons of *Humble Influence* resonate deeply in such moments. They remind us that followership is not passive compliance but an active, intentional choice to align with a mission, support leadership, and contribute meaningfully. These principles can transform every aspect of life, from careers to families, faith communities to volunteer roles.

Followership in the Workplace

In her office, Sarah thought about how followership could change her perspective. She saw how being a reliable, adaptable team member strengthened her department's cohesion. When she took initiative—anticipating challenges and solving problems without waiting for her manager's direction—she felt more engaged and purposeful.

In the workplace, followership creates a foundation for success. By supporting leaders through critical thinking and proactive efforts, employees amplify the team's achievements. Sarah's newfound perspective led her to excel in her role, and over time, she became a trusted resource for her manager and peers.

The Influence of Followership in Families

Later that week, Sarah reflected on how followership applied at home. As the oldest sibling, she often felt the need to lead her family through challenges. But she realized that following her parents' guidance with humility was just as important. Supporting her younger siblings by being present and encouraging mirrored the biblical principle of serving others selflessly.

Within families, followership fosters stronger bonds. It teaches humility, patience, and the value of prioritizing others' needs. Sarah saw how following well helped her family flourish, deepening their love and unity.

Following in Church and Community

On Sunday, Sarah returned to church, where she volunteered as part of the children's ministry team. She noticed how small acts of service—cleaning classrooms, preparing crafts, and teaching Bible lessons—had a ripple effect. The children's joy and curiosity were reminders that her efforts mattered.

In faith communities, followership is often an act of worship. It aligns with the calling to serve others, just as Christ demonstrated throughout His life. For Sarah, this brought a sense of spiritual fulfillment, knowing her work contributed to something eternal.

Volunteer Boards and Leadership Teams

Sarah was also part of her neighborhood's community board. She'd struggled with balancing her desire to contribute ideas with her frustration at being overshadowed by louder voices. But as she applied the principles of *Humble Influence,* Sarah found power in listening and aligning with the group's mission. By supporting the board's goals and offering thoughtful insights, she became an integral part of the team's success.

Through this, Sarah learned that effective followers aren't focused on recognition. They strive to support a collective mission, taking initiative where needed and collaborating with others. Her efforts helped the board secure funding for a local park renovation—an achievement that benefited the entire community.

The Fulfillment of Purpose-Driven Followership

As Sarah reflected on the changes in her life, she noticed a deep sense of fulfillment. Following with humility and intention allowed her to see the impact of her contributions. She wasn't just completing tasks; she was serving a purpose. Her work and relationships felt more meaningful, and she realized she was building a legacy of service and collaboration.

Followership as a Path to Significance and Success

Over time, Sarah's approach to followership prepared her for leadership opportunities. When her manager took a sabbatical, Sarah stepped in to lead a major project. Her years of supporting the team and honing her skills paid off—she navigated the challenges with confidence, earning the trust of her colleagues.

Her story mirrors a timeless truth: those who master followership gain the skills and character needed to lead effectively. By embracing humility, aligning with a mission, and contributing selflessly, Sarah found success, fulfillment, and significance.

Sarah's journey reflects the heart of *Humble Influence*: that true greatness lies not in seeking the spotlight but in serving with purpose. Followership is the foundation for all impactful work—whether in careers, families, faith communities, or beyond. It teaches us that every role matters, every effort contributes, and every follower has the potential to lead with grace when the time comes.

Followership is the new leadership. It's time we celebrate the unsung heroes—the followers who work diligently, think critically, and act courageously. You are now part of this **Humble Influence Movement**, a collective of individuals who understand that great teams, organizations, and communities are built not by leaders alone but by the efforts of those who follow with purpose.

Thank you for joining this journey. As you continue to grow and contribute, remember this: ***You don't have to lead to make a difference.*** Follow with intent, act with courage, and leave a legacy that inspires others to do the same.

The future isn't shaped by leaders alone—it's shaped by followers like you.

ADDITIONAL RESOURCES

Visit humbleinfluencebook.com
for free videos and other bonus content.

HUMBLE INFLUENCE ROADMAP TO BECOMING AN EFFECTIVE FOLLOWER

Adopt a Servant Mindset- embrace humility and recognize that effective followership is about contributing to the greater good, not personal gain. Serve your leader, team, and mission with dedication and selflessness.

Understand the Mission- align your efforts with the organization's goals and purpose. Seek clarity about the leader's vision and how your role fits into the bigger picture.

Cultivate Key Traits:

- *Humility-* serve without seeking the spotlight.
- *Curiosity-* seek to understand before seeking to be understood; ask questions, explore new perspectives, and remain open to continuous learning.
- *Courage-* offer constructive feedback and respectfully challenge decisions when necessary.
- *Loyalty-* stay committed to the mission, especially during challenging times.
- *Proactivity-* take initiative and contribute beyond assigned tasks.
- *Learn through observation-* study the successes, challenges, and decisions of leaders and peers to gain insights that can shape your own approach.

Communicate effectively- keep open and transparent communication with your leader. Provide updates, voice concerns constructively, and share ideas to support the team's success.

Take responsibility- own your tasks and deliver results consistently. Be dependable, reliable, and accountable for your contributions.

Embrace continuous growth- see followership as a phase of personal and professional development. Seek feedback, learn new skills, and adapt to evolving challenges.

Support and empower leadership- strengthen your leader's efforts by filling gaps, anticipating needs, and offering solutions. Work collaboratively, showing empathy and understanding the pressures of leadership.

Focus on collective success- celebrate team achievements and prioritize the organization's goals over individual recognition.

Reflect on your purpose- regularly reconnect with your "why" to stay motivated and aligned with your values.

HUMBLE INFLUENCE ROAD MAP TO
BECOMING AN EFFECTIVE FOLLOWER

Cultivate Key Traits

Humility- serve without seeking the spotlight.
Curiosity- seek to understand before seeking to be understood; ask questions, explore new perspectives, and remain open to continuous learning.
Courage - offer constructive feedback and respectfully challenge decisions when necessary.
Loyalty- stay committed to the mission, especially during challenging times.
Proactivity-take initiative and contribute beyond assigned tasks.
Observation- study the success, challenges, and decisions of leaders and peers to gain insights that can shape your own approach.

Understand the Mission

Align your efforts with the organizations' goals and purpose. Seek clarity about the leader's vision and how your role fits into the bigger picture.

Communicate Effectively

Keep open and transparent communication with your leader.

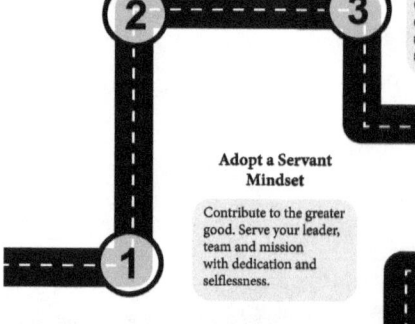

Adopt a Servant Mindset

Contribute to the greater good. Serve your leader, team and mission with dedication and selflessness.

Take Responsibility

Own your tasks and deliver results consistently.

Support and Empower Leadership

Strengthen your leader's efforts by filling gaps, anticipating needs, offering solutions, working collaboratively, showing empathy & understanding the pressures of leadership.

Reflect on Your Purpose

Regularly reconnect with your why to stay motivated and aligned with your values.

Focus on Collective Success

Celebrate team achievements and prioritize the organization's goals over individual recognition.

Embrace Continuous Growth

Seek feedback, learn new skills, and adapt to evolving challenges.

Visit humbleinfluencebook.com for a free downloadable PDF.

EXERCISES TO FIND YOUR WHY

Purpose Mapping
Create a chart with three columns: **What I'm good at... What I enjoy doing... How I help others...**
List all the things that come to mind. Look for overlaps to identify your "why."

The 5 Whys Technique
Start with a statement about your work and ask "why" five times.

An example: I design apps.
>   *Why?* To make life easier for users.
>   *Why?* Because I want to solve real problems.
>   *Why?* To create value in people's lives.
>   *Why?* I enjoy designing.
>   *Why?* I can make an impact in the world.

Gratitude Reflection
At the end of each day, write down one thing you're grateful for in your work. Over time, patterns will emerge that point to your purpose.

SELF-ASSESSMENT: FOLLOWERSHIP SKILLS

Instructions- Rate yourself on a scale of 1–5 (1 = Needs Improvement, 5 = Excellent) for each skill. Reflect on your scores and set goals for improvement.

Communication

I actively listen and seek to understand   1   2   3   4   5
my leader's and team's needs.

I share insights and feedback   1   2   3   4   5
constructively and respectfully.

Goal(s) for Improvement:

Collaboration

I prioritize team success over personal   1   2   3   4   5
recognition.

I work well with diverse personalities   1   2   3   4   5
and perspectives.

Goal(s) for Improvement:

Initiative

I identify problems and offer solutions without waiting for direction.   1   2   3   4   5

I take ownership of my responsibilities and follow through consistently.   1   2   3   4   5

Goal(s) for Improvement:

Judgment

I provide thoughtful, evidence-based feedback when appropriate.   1   2   3   4   5

I balance constructive criticism with respect for leadership.   1   2   3   4   5

Goal(s) for Improvement:

Authenticity

I bring my true self to work and align my actions with my values.   1   2   3   4   5

I embrace my unique strengths and contribute them to the team.   1   2   3   4   5

Goal(s) for Improvement:

VALUES ALIGNMENT EXERCISE

Write down your top three values (e.g., honesty, collaboration, innovation).

1. _____
2. _____
3. _____

Reflect on how these values align with your organization's mission and your current role.

Identify one action you can take this week to better live out these values in your work.

TEAM ACKNOWLEDGEMENT CHALLENGE

Choose one team member each day to recognize for their contributions. Be specific- mention what they did and how it impacted the team or mission.

Monday
*who:*_____ *what:*_____

Tuesday
*who:*_____ *what:*_____

Wednesday
*who:*_____ *what:*_____

Thursday
*who:*_____ *what:*_____

Friday
*who:*_____ *what:*_____

*At the end of the week, reflect on how this practice affected:

Team morale-

Your relationships-

PERSONAL EMPOWERMENT PLAN

Identify an area in your work where you'd like more responsibility.

Develop a proposal outlining your ideas and how they align with the organization's goals.

My Idea
  1. What it is
    a.
    b.
    c.

  2. Why it is needed in the organization
    a.
    b.
    c.

  3. How it can be implemented in the organization
    a.
    b.
    c.

Present your proposal to your leader with confidence and humility.

FOLLOWERSHIP TOOLKIT

Feedback Journal Template

Date:
Feedback Received:
Reflection: *How can I apply this feedback to grow?*
Action Plan: *What steps will I take to improve?*
    1.
    2.
    3.

Personal Improvement Plan

Skill to Improve:
Current Status: *Where do I stand today?*
Goal: *What do I want to achieve?*
Action Steps:
    1.
    2.
    3.
    Timeline: *By when will I achieve this?*

Followership Principles Checklist
Did I align my work with the team's mission today?
Did I take initiative and contribute beyond my job description?
Did I communicate openly and effectively with my leader and peers?
Did I celebrate others' contributions and share credit where appropriate?
Did I bring my authentic self to my work today?

Personal Growth Prompts
Use these prompts to guide your personal growth as a follower.

Daily Reflection
What did I do today to support my leader or team?
Did I focus on the mission, or did personal concerns distract me?

Weekly Reflection
How did I use my strengths to contribute this week?
Was there a time when I should have spoken up but didn't? What held me back?

Monthly Reflection
What feedback have I received, and how have I applied it?
How have I demonstrated initiative and accountability this month?

Final Thought: This toolkit is a starting point for your journey as an empowered, effective follower. Whether you use these resources for personal growth, team development, or organizational transformation, remember: *followership is a skill that can elevate not only your work but the success of those around you.*

ABOUT THE AUTHOR

Jim Matuga is a seasoned entrepreneur, business leader, and community advocate with over thirty years of experience helping organizations and individuals thrive. He is the founder of InnerAction Media, a West Virginia-based marketing agency, and Positively West Virginia, a podcast and media platform dedicated to showcasing and celebrating the innovative spirit, resilience, and entrepreneurial success stories of West Virginia business leaders.

Through his work with InnerAction Media and Positively West Virginia, Jim has built a reputation as a trusted voice for businesses, nonprofits, and community leaders. His efforts have been instrumental in crafting compelling strategies, telling authentic stories, and inspiring action that drives measurable results.

Jim's career has been shaped by a deep commitment to service, collaboration, and mentorship. He has had the privilege of working with and learning from some of the most influential leaders of his time, including Milan Puskar, founder of Mylan Laboratories, and Doug Leech, founder of Centra Bank. These experiences have given him a unique perspective on the critical, often overlooked role of followership in achieving lasting success.

As a passionate advocate for leadership development, Jim has spent decades observing how great followership supports great leadership. His firsthand experiences in business and his role as a mentor have shown him that followership is not a passive role but an active, essential force in any successful endeavor.

With Positively West Virginia, Jim has amplified the voices of entrepreneurs and leaders across his home state, further solidifying his mission to empower individuals and organizations to embrace their full potential.

As a speaker, writer, and trusted advisor, Jim combines timeless wisdom with practical strategies to help others lead, serve, and succeed with purpose. His work is rooted in the belief that the most impactful leaders are those who first learn to follow with humility, intention, and dedication.

When Jim isn't mentoring future leaders, promoting West Virginia's inspiring stories, or guiding businesses to success, he enjoys exploring the scenic beauty of his home state, serving his community, and cherishing time with his wife Rebekah and his family.

Jim Matuga invites you to join the movement to redefine followership and discover its transformative power in every area of life.

Jim
MATUGA

Author of books
Humble Influence
Marketing Matters
Physical Therapy Rocket Fuel

Host of
Positively West Virginia podcast

Available for
Speaking Opportunities,
Coaching and Consulting

Connect with Jim

Contact
jim@inneractionmedia.com

We tell compelling marketing stories for companies and non-profit organizations.

Video Production

Digital, Traditional and Social Media Advertising

Web Site Development

inner**action**media

Contact: Jim Matuga
jim@inneractionmedia.com
(304) 241-4959

A Christ-centered sanctuary for girls education and family restoration

REFUGE
Mountain Ranch

Located on 350 beautiful acres
in Western Maryland,
RMR provides education, healing and love
to girls in crisis to reclaim their lives, discover
their worth, and walk in faith
with Jesus Christ.

Portion of the profits from *Humble Influence* support Refuge Mountain Ranch

Contact: refugemountainranch.org | (240) 727-5142

www.ingramcontent.com/pod-product-compliance
Lightning Source LLC
Chambersburg PA
CBHW031525120626
46545CB00005B/2011